Prepare your child for school

PREPARE YOUR CHILD

For School

A PARENTS' HANDBOOK

CLARE SHAW

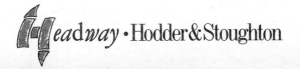

Headway · Hodder & Stoughton

Cataloguing in Publication Data is available from the British Library

ISBN 0-340-60797-1

First published 1994
Impression number   10 9 8 7 6 5 4 3 2 1
Year   1998 1997 1996 1995 1994

Typeset by Rowland Phototypesetting Limited, Bury St Edmunds, Suffolk.
Printed in Great Britain for the educational publishing division of Hodder Headline
Plc, 338 Euston Road, London NW1 3BH by Cox and Wyman Limited, Reading.

Positive Parenting

Positive Parenting is a series of handbooks primarily written for parents, in a clear, accessible style, giving practical information, sound advice and sources of specialist and general help. Based on the authors' extensive professional and personal experience, they cover a wide range of topics and provide an invaluable source of encouragement and information to all who are involved in child care in the home and in the community.

Other books in this series include:

Talking and your child by Clare Shaw – a guide outlining the details of how speech and language develops from birth to age 11 and how parents can help with the process.

Your child from 5–11 by Jennie and Lance Lindon – a guide showing parents how they can help their children through these crucial early years, stressing the contribution a caring family can make to the emotional, physical and intellectual development of the child.

Your child with special needs by Susan Kerr – a guide for the parents of the one-in-five children with special needs, giving families practical advice and emotional support, based on the shared experiences of other parents.

Help your child through school by Jennie and Lance Lindon – a guide which looks at the school years from the perspective of the family, showing how parents can help their children to get the most out of their years at primary school and how to ease the transition into secondary education.

Coming soon

Help your child with maths (July 1994)

Help your child with reading and writing (July 1994)

Help your child with a foreign languge (July 1994)

Whereas the authors of this series have offered ideas and practical suggestions in the light of their own experience and knowledge, only parents have the personal knowledge of their own family and children to enable them to make a sensible decision about what they will try and what could be best for them.

N.B. In **Preparing your child for school** the author has used 'he' and 'she' in alternate paragraphs.

Contents

1   Ready for school – what does it mean?   1

2   Two years to go – getting your three- to
    four-year-old ready   13

3   One year to go – getting your four- to
    five-year-old ready   30

4   Helping your child with goodbyes   46

5   Help yourself – steps to independence   59

6   Pay attention – helping your child to listen   69

7   Toys and equipment – what to buy and make   81

8   Making friends – good social skills and
    behaviour   92

9   Which pre-school group?   107

10 Ready for the three Rs   119

11 Which school?   131

12 Ready or not?   144

13 Starting school – the first term   153

    Useful addresses   168

    Index   170

About the authors

Clare Shaw is a working Speech and Language Therapist with a special interest in pre-school children. Author of **Talking and your child**, she also writes extensively for parenting magazines. She is a parent herself with two young daughters.

Acknowledgements

Thank you to all parents and professionals who contributed to the book with their expertise and experience.

Particular thanks to Carol White, Lindsay Kennedy, Colin Watson, Linda Miles and all the other parents of pre-school and primary children who filled in questionnaires.

To the early stages teachers in the Grampian region, especially Sheila Johnston, and the nursery teachers and playgroup leaders of Aberdeen.

Health visitors: Isobel Milne, Gillian Grant and Beth Struthers, for their expertise and support.

Geoff Jones and Robert Macdonald, for their in-depth knowledge of child development and paediatrics.

John Burgess, for his continued support and enthusiasm, and Jessica and Emma, the two I prepared myself.

CHAPTER ONE

Ready for school – what does it mean?

That very first day at school is a memorable milestone for both parent and child. Whatever your child's pre-school experience has been – whether it involves both parents working, staying at home, full- or part-time nursery, playgroup or time with a child-minder – starting school is undoubtedly a big step forward. But a big step forward does not have to be a step into the unknown, fraught with fear, anxiety and inability to cope. It should be something which both parent and child look forward to with knowledge, confidence and excitement.

Many of us will remember our own very first day at school and those with older children already in full-time education will certainly remember theirs. Whether this is a happy memory to look back on with pride or an occasion we would rather forget will depend on how prepared we were. And, of course, being prepared for school does not just involve your child. The whole family needs to be prepared for the big day.

Preparation necessarily involves the confidence which comes from knowing exactly what is involved. Both you and your child should know so much about the school and what is going to happen that by day one, you will feel that he has been going there for months already. Your child should have the confidence to face something new and this will be helped by ability. Ability to do all the things that will be expected of him, from hanging up his coat to asking for the toilet. He should also be reassured that he does not need to know *everything* and that teachers and friends, including some familiar faces, will be there to help him.

A well-prepared child is more likely to settle in quickly, be happy and relaxed and build up relationships easily with both teachers and children. A well-prepared child will be ready to continue the learning process which has already started at home and nursery or playgroup. A well-prepared parent can help and support their child during those first few important weeks. So do not let that first school day creep up on you suddenly. If you plan ahead carefully, you really will be able to turn up at the school gates, proudly announcing 'And here's one I prepared earlier . . . !'.

When does it all start?

In one sense, preparing your child for school starts when she is a baby. Right from the start, you are helping your child cope without you – you put toys in her cot so that she can entertain herself. You will be helping your child get to know other adults, whether it is Grandma, the babysitter or the child-minder. You will then find yourself helping your toddler eat independently, ask for what she needs and use the toilet by herself. Later you will be encouraging your child to share and take turns and to become part of a bigger group of children, perhaps at nursery or playgroup. Without even realising it, you are gradually teaching your child the skills and independence she will need when she starts school.

Before the age of three, this preparation will be more or less unconscious – school itself will seem a life-time away. At three, though, you will be thinking about some form of pre-school education. If both parents (or one single parent) are working, you may feel that the nanny or child-minder will not be sufficient in preparing your child and that a bigger group of children is more appropriate. In considering nursery, or perhaps playgroup for families with a parent at home, you are making school preparation much more deliberate.

Once your child is in her final year as a pre-schooler, you will need to think about very specific tasks and skills which your child will need and then school preparation is really under way.

Who is involved?

Your child

Your child is obviously involved in getting ready for school even though it may be the parents who are most nervous! Of course, you will not be talking very specifically about school until a few months before he starts. However, if you are going to teach your child particular skills such as getting dressed and washing his hands independently, he has got to *want* to succeed – you cannot do it all for him. You can help build up his motivation with a lot of praise and encouragement, perhaps even with rewards.

Parents

Whether or not your child goes to a nursery or playgroup, parents are still the most important people when it comes to getting him ready. You will have all the practicalities to deal with from choosing a school to registering your child and ensuring he has a visit there before school starts. You will also need to talk to him about school before he begins and deal with any questions or anxieties he may have. You can use the checklist in this chapter to ensure that he has the necessary skills to go to school with confidence.

Other children

Your child would be very nervous going into the classroom if she was not used to other children, especially a reasonably large group of them. She will be best prepared if she has attended a nursery school or playgroup. It would be little help though, if your child has not used this pre-school experience to make friends, gradually playing *with* other children rather than just alongside them. Being with other children should help your child acquire those essential social skills of sharing and taking turns. If you know of other girls and boys who will be starting school with your child, you might encourage friendships by inviting them round to your home. Some familiar faces at school are bound to help your child settle in.

Other family and friends

Other children in the family can be very involved in helping a child get ready. If they are already at school, they will be able to provide all sorts of inside information. Make sure that this is positive (and truthful) though. If the brother or sister is much older, and going through an 'I hate school' phase, he is more likely to tell horror stories of what might be in the school dinners or what Mrs Macpherson did to poor Sally Dobbs. What you really want a younger child to hear is what fun it is and how nice the teachers (and dinners) are. If you are friendly with other parents who already have children at school or about to start they and their children can provide an excellent source of support.

If all this being prepared makes you feel as if you have just joined some kind of scout troop, remember that in a way you have. There is a whole troop of parents out there who are going through or have already been through the same as you, so get talking and support each other. And the more families you get together with, the more familiar faces there will be in the playground and in the classroom.

If your child spends a lot of time with other relatives, perhaps grandparents, have a chat with them as school approaches. It is important that you all have the same positive attitude and do not give your child conflicting information.

Nursery and playgroup teachers

One of the roles, some might say *the* role, of nurseries and play-groups is to prepare children for school. Sometimes there is a direct link between the nursery or playgroup and the school, particularly if they both take place in the same or adjacent buildings. In this instance, school teachers may visit the nursery or playgroup and the children may have several visits to the school. In some more formal nurseries, the teacher even sends a written report on each child to the head of the appropriate school.

In any pre-school group, children will get used to being part of that group and learn to cope with the practicalities from washing hands to handling a cup of juice. Most pre-school groups will incorporate activities which then continue at school. These include painting, cutting and sticking, singing and action games. Some pre-school groups also include more formal pre-reading and pre-writing activities.

Health visitors

Health visitors will have monitored your child's development from an early age. They will have carried out regular development checks including a pre-school assessment, which will usually take place during the six months prior to starting school. Health visitors will screen for specific problems such as hearing loss, sight defects and delayed speech and language development and will refer your child to any relevant specialists if necessary. They will advise you about the ins and outs of starting school itself and answer any questions you have.

The school

The head of the school your child will be attending, and probably her first teacher, will ensure that they have met your child before she actually starts. This enables your child to be more familiar with the teacher and the surroundings and gives the teacher the opportunity to get to know her a little. Sometimes, strong links are established between the school and local pre-school groups and this makes the transition between pre-school and school very smooth indeed.

Aims of preparing for school

- To give your child a positive attitude to school.
- To ensure that she will look forward to it and then enjoy it.
- To ensure that your child will be able to relate to the other children.
- To help your child relate well to the teachers.
- To give your child confidence with the routine activities she will encounter.
- To ensure that she will have the emotional and practical independence to cope without you.
- To make sure that she understands what will happen when she gets there.
- To enable teachers to be aware of any individual problems or characteristics.
- To create opportunities to discuss school entry with your child in a positive and enjoyable way.
- To ensure that your child reaches her potential.

Not the aims

- To teach your child to read or write before she starts school.

READY FOR SCHOOL – WHAT DOES IT MEAN?

- To make sure that she is ahead of the other children.
- To warn her that if she does not work hard and do as the teacher says then she will not get any sweets after school or a job later in life.
- To give a big build up to the first day, starting months or even years before the event.
- To change the subject when school is mentioned and talk about it as little as possible for fear of upsetting your child.
- To use school or the teacher as a threat.
- To teach your child to count up to a hundred or recite the alphabet.
- To teach your child to stand up for herself, perhaps by hitting back.
- To make sure that your child never cries.
- To make sure that your child has the best crayons, the newest clothes and the biggest lunch box.

AT A GLANCE CHECKLIST
What your child should be doing before school entry

Talking (chapters 2 and 3)

Your child should be able to:

- make himself understood;
- ask for what he needs, answer simple questions and relate what he has done during the day;
- know the names of the primary colours, his name and address;
- use his communication skills to build up good relationships with other children and the teacher;
- stop talking and listen.

Understanding (chapters 2 and 3)

Your child should be able to:

- follow simple instructions likely to be given in the classroom;
- understand and enjoy a simple story;
- understand different types of questions including those beginning with 'Why?';
- understand what numbers mean, count objects out up to four or five and rote count even further;
- understand most of what is said to her and ask when she does not.

Play (chapters 2, 3 and 7)

Your child should be able to:

- take turns most of the time;
- show some signs of being able to share;
- play *with* other children meaningfully, which will include two-way communication;
- use pretend play with small toys such as play people; pretend objects are something else and pretend he himself is something or somebody else;
- play with a toy for longer than ten minutes.

Physical development and movement (chapters 2 and 3)

Your child should be able to:

- ride a tricycle with ease;
- hop on one leg;
- walk or run on tiptoe;
- catch and throw a large ball with reasonable accuracy;
- walk along a narrow line, placing one foot in front of another.

Small movements and visual skills (chapters 2 and 3)

Your child should be able to:

- thread beads;
- build a tower of ten bricks;
- hold a pencil with an adult grip (usually) and use it in a controlled way. She should be able to copy simple shapes and draw a recognisable man;
- colour pictures in, within the lines;
- pick up a crumb between her thumb and forefinger.

Social skills (chapters 2, 3, and 8)

Your child should be able to:

- form friendships, play with other children and show some understanding of the feelings of others;
- realise that certain behaviour is unacceptable;
- know how to use the toilet, eat a meal properly and use a hanky;
- refrain from using excessive aggression, arguing with words more than with physical strength;
- talk and behave appropriately in front of adults.

Independence (chapters 4 and 5)

Your child should be able to:

- say goodbye to you happily, secure in the knowledge that you will be back at the end of the day;
- allow other familiar adults to help him;
- dress and undress with minimal help;
- eat a meal with minimal help;
- use a toilet, wash his hands and blow his nose independently.

Pre-reading skills (chapter 10)

Your child should know:

- that a book starts at the front, finishes at the back and that words run from left to right;
- that a written word means something and can be read;
- her own name when she sees it written down;
- that stories are interesting and reading them exciting;
- how to tell a story from looking at the pictures.

Pre-writing skills (chapter 10)

Your child should be able to:

- hold a pencil with a mature grasp and control its movements;
- copy shapes and perhaps some of the easier letters;
- colour in and trace a picture;
- use pretend writing which goes from left to right;
- draw recognisable pictures.

Listening and concentration (chapter 6)

Your child should be able to:

- stop what he is doing when he hears his name;
- concentrate on a game or task for more than ten minutes;
- listen to a story which lasts for at least ten minutes, with interest and enjoyment;
- attempt to complete most tasks he starts, whether a book, puzzle, drawing or whatever;
- remember the words to familiar rhymes and songs.

Safety (chapters 5 and 13)

Your child should know:

- how to cross the road safely;
- what to do in the unlikely event that you are not waiting at the school gate;
- what to do if approached by a stranger;
- what to do if a familiar adult makes her feel uncomfortable;
- what to do in the event of a fire – and that matches are dangerous.

Exceptions to the rule

Children are all different and develop at their own rate. Children do not all say their first words at exactly 13 months, two weeks and one day for example, although this may be a near average. Similarly, children starting school will all have their own strengths and weaknesses. The most important thing is to know *your* child and have reasonable expectations for her. The checklist cannot, therefore, be taken as a pass/fail list but should just be used as a guideline. Your child is not going to fail at school or be desperately unhappy if she still finds one or two of the items tricky when she begins. Some children may be positively dangerous when wielding a knife and fork, for example, while others may still be mastering their colours. The important thing is to identify any weak areas, but not so that you can push your child on quickly to ensure they are mastered before the first day of term. Instead, you can gently encourage your child in these areas and, if necessary, tell the teacher which items she still finds difficult.

Ready for more?

You may find that your child is ready for school well before the start of term and raring to get going on reading and writing, for example. Remember that the age of children starting school does vary, albeit by only a few months. But the difference between a four-and-a-half-year-old and a five-year-old at this stage can be enormous. It could be, therefore, that your child has passed, or is approaching, her fifth birthday and is very able in some areas. You will not, of course, want to push your child too hard but neither will you want to hold her back. You could consider doing some more formal teaching, perhaps using some of the ideas in chapter 10 on 'Getting ready for the three Rs'. Remember, however, that the three Rs are only a part of school life. Check that your child is developing in other areas too, such as social skills or self-help skills.

Always take the lead from your child. You may feel that she is ready to read but if she makes it clear that she is just not interested, make sure you do not put her off. Instead of pushing on with reading, spend time building up her interest in books and stories so that she will really want to read. When she wants to do it, and shows you that she can learn, you can discuss it with her pre-school group or the school she will be attending. The teachers may make some suggestions on how you can help at home. Other ideas are outlined in detail throughout this book. Just remember to encourage your child in *all* areas of development and most of all, have fun!

Two years to go – getting your three- to four-year-old ready

When your child is three, school will seem a long way off and it will seem far too early to start preparing for it. But you are probably preparing your child for school without even realising it! As long as you are aware of your child's level of development and are helping her with the next step; and while you are encouraging your child to socialise with other children, she will be taking another step towards being ready for school. It is worth taking some time really to observe your child and see just what she can and cannot do in all areas of development. Large and fine movements, communication and understanding, play and social skills will all be developing rapidly and you can encourage and help that development with games and activities for you both to enjoy. Remember too that one skill leads to another – manipulative skills are really pre-writing skills and communication is an essential skill for learning to read.

Enjoy the activities together, remembering to let your child take the lead from time to time, stepping back to let her experiment and develop imaginative skills on her own.

Physical development and movement

Your three- to four-year-old should be able to:

- walk up and down stairs, although some children may still keep two feet to a step;
- jump from the bottom step;
- attempt the ladder on the slide in the park;
- run around corners, avoiding obstacles;
- walk backwards;
- ride a tricycle, steering it competently;
- walk on tiptoe;
- stand on one foot;
- throw and kick a ball;
- catch a large ball with arms held outstretched.

Move it games

Ball games

Your child will enjoy throwing and catching a ball although you need to use a large one and throw it gently to start with. If he finds this difficult try using a large bean bag which is easier to grip. Improvise a goal and see if your child can kick a ball between the 'posts'. Play ball with the whole family, making it into a game by shouting out the person's name before you throw it to them. Or give everyone a number or colour and shout that out first. Hang up a large hoop from a tree and see if your child can throw a ball through it.

Foot-in-front obstacle course

Make an obstacle course out of planks, logs and lengths of thick rope. The idea is to encourage your child to put one foot in front of the other to walk along the obstacles. Good balance is needed for this activity. Turn it into a game by telling children that they have to get over the bridge without falling into the shark-infested water.

Swimming

Your child should be going swimming by now and feel confident in the water, although he does not yet need to be able to swim. Encourage your child to move his arms in a doggy-paddle fashion and kick his legs – you can even practise these movements in the bath. Take a floating toy to the pool with you for your child to swim towards and reach out for. It requires good co-ordination to grab it while swimming.

Tricycle course

Put out skittles (or empty plastic bottles) for your child to cycle between and around without knocking them over. Make a bridge for her to go under so she has to cycle and bend her head down at the same time.

Potato and spoon race

See if your child can run or walk quickly while holding a spoon with a potato in it. Invite his friends round and have a 'sports' afternoon.

Manipulation

Your three- to four-year-old should be able to:

- pick up something as small as a crumb between his thumb and first finger;
- build a tower of eight or nine bricks;
- thread wooden beads on to a lace;
- cut with scissors – although some children may not do this very effectively yet;
- hold a pencil and copy a circle and a cross;
- colour in a picture fairly accurately;
- do velcro fastenings up. Some children manage large buttons;
- turn a tap on and off;
- hold one finger up at a time, although third and fourth fingers may be difficult;
- draw round a shape – although some help may be needed.

Finger games

Fun finger rhymes

Try finger rhymes to get manipulation going. The following four are good ones to start you off:

Tommy Thumb, Tommy Thumb, where are you?
(*clench your fist*)
Here I am, here I am.
(*stick your thumb up*)
How do you do?
(*bend your thumb over*)

TWO YEARS TO GO

Repeat this rhyme using your other fingers – Peter Pointer (index finger), Toby Tall (middle finger), Ruby Ring (ring finger) and Baby Small (little finger).

Two fat gentlemen met in the lane,
(*hold both thumbs up facing each other*)
Bowed most politely, bowed once again.
(*bend your thumbs twice*)
How do you do, how do you do, how do you do again?
(*bend your thumbs three times*)

Repeat this rhyme using your other fingers – two thin ladies (index fingers), two tall policemen (middle fingers), two cheeky school boys (ring fingers) and two little babies (little fingers).

Incy Wincy Spider climbed up the water spout,
(*touch your little fingers with the thumbs of your opposite hands in a climbing and twisting action*)
Down came the rain and washed the spider out.
(*wriggle your fingers like drops of rain falling*)
Out came the sun and dried up all the rain.
(*make a circle by putting the tips of your fingers and thumbs together*)
Incy Wincy Spider climbed up the spout again.
(*repeat the climbing action*)

Here are Mummy's knives and forks,
(*hold your hands back to back, fingers facing upwards and interlocking*)
Here is Mummy's table,
(*turn your hands over so your fingers point downwards, and drop your wrists down*)

PREPARE YOUR CHILD FOR SCHOOL

Here is Mummy's mirror now,
(*stick up your two first fingers, touching at the tips*)
And here is baby's cradle.
(*put your little fingers up and rock hands*)

Creative collage

Your child may find cutting round pictures very difficult when she first starts to use scissors. Collect together some sheets of coloured paper, silver foil and old wrapping paper so that she can cut out shapes more randomly. If she sticks these on to a larger sheet of paper or card, she can make a very effective collage. Once she can do this well, see if your child can cut along straight lines. Perhaps she could cut some marked sheets of newspaper up into strips for dunking into glue for papier mâché. Next she will be ready to cut around pictures so keep all your old catalogues and magazines for this.

Finger painting

If you mix dry powder paint or food colouring with wallpaper paste (non-fungicidal), this makes a good thick, smooth paint for finger painting. Put lots of blobs of different coloured paint in the centre of a large piece of thick paper. Now get your child to spread it around with his fingers to make patterns. For really exact manipulative skills, see if he can use a different finger for each colour.

Pick-a-straw

Take a packet of coloured straws and hold them vertically in a bunch with your hand resting on the table or floor. Let go so that they all fall in a heap, then take it in turns to pick them up carefully, one at a time, without moving the others. You could collect a colour each to make it more difficult.

Pipe cleaner people

Pipe cleaners are ideal for encouraging manipulative play and can be used on their own or put through straws to make them bendy. You could make up a story about a visit to the zoo and help your child to make the accompanying people and animals.

Communication

Your three- to four-year-old should be able to:

- use sentences of at least four words;
- use a vocabulary of 1,000 words;
- ask for what she needs even if some little words are omitted and grammar is sometimes immature;
- tell you her full name, sex, age and sometimes the town and street she lives in;
- use some position words – 'in', 'on', 'next to', etc.
- sing many nursery rhymes with few mistakes;
- ask questions, particularly those beginning with 'What?', 'Where?' and 'Who?'. Listen to the answers;
- use words which represent people, i.e. 'I' or 'me', 'you', 'she', 'he', 'it', 'his', 'her', etc. (by three-and-a-half to four);
- talk about past, present and future (by three-and-a-half to four);
- enjoy conversation with adults and other children.

Talking games

What's wrong?

Children of this age love pictures or stories with deliberate mistakes. Draw pictures of people with wellington boots on their heads or a banana coming out of their ear and get your child to tell you what is wrong. Now see if he can think of any funny pictures for you to draw.

You can do the same thing with stories. You start by saying something like 'Mr Daft had a plate of shoes for breakfast' and then encourage your child to join in with what he might have had for dinner.

Feely bag

Put some objects into a bag and take it in turns to put your hands in, feel one and then describe it for the other person to guess. When it is your turn to give the clues, your child may just shout out guesses as to what she thinks it is. But demonstrate when you have *your* turn how to use describing words – 'It's long and hard' or 'It's soft and squidgy' and so on. To start with, make it easier by letting your child see all the objects first, as you put them into the bag.

Picture stories

Think of an everyday sequence such as getting up in the morning or posting a letter, and divide it in to four or five steps. For example, going to bed could involve getting undressed, having a bath, cleaning teeth, putting pyjamas on and getting into bed. With your child, draw a picture to represent each step on to separate cards. Now see if he can put them in the right order and tell you the story.

Diary scrap book

This is very useful if your child spends a lot of time with a nanny, child-minder or grandparent. So often, at this age, when someone asks your child what she has been doing, the automatic response is 'Don't know' or even 'Nothing'. Now she can take her scrap book with her and show Grandma exactly what she has been up to. So every time you go on a trip or just out for a walk, draw a picture about what you have been doing and stick in any interesting leaves, bus tickets or lolly sticks.

Puppet shows

Puppets are excellent for encouraging conversation – they can be made to talk to each other or you can act out a familiar story together. Choose stories with repetitive lines to start with – 'I'll huff and I'll puff and I'll blow your house down' or 'Run, run as fast as you can, you can't catch me I'm the gingerbread man'. Soon your child will be making up his own words. You do not have to buy expensive glove puppets – use old socks with buttons sewn on for eyes or paper bags with faces drawn on.

Understanding

Your three- to four-year-old should be able to:

- follow and enjoy short stories in books;
- understand your questions ('Why?' questions may still be hard);
- understand many size words ('big', 'little', 'fat', 'short');
- understand position words – 'in', 'on', 'under', 'behind';
- know some of the rules of grammar (Say, 'Today I bup, yesterday I . . .' and your child will say 'bupped' even though it is nonsense.);
- understand negatives – 'no', 'not', 'never', 'none';
- follow a conversation about past events;
- follow a conversation about future events;
- follow pre-school television programmes;
- understand simple instructions such as 'Come in and wash your hands'.

Games for understanding

Give us a clue

Cut a selection of pictures out of a magazine and put them on the table. Now give your child some clues to see if she can select the right one. So for a bicycle, you could say 'It's got wheels and you sit on it' or for a teddy bear, 'It's soft and yellow and you take it to bed'. To make this more difficult, see if you child can guess what you are describing without seeing the pictures first.

Treasure hunt

Give your child a clue for finding the treasure – something like, 'It's under something you sit on' or 'It's in the room next to the kitchen, underneath the towel'. To make the game longer, each clue could lead to another one which your child brings to you to read out.

Here we go round

You do not have to stick to the script when you sing action songs with your child. Try 'Here we go round the Mulberry Bush' but when you say 'This is the way we . . .' just mime an action and see if your child can guess what the mine is. Then let him have a go at miming.

Listening obstacle course

Put out some obstacles in the garden or lounge and then give your child instructions before she tackles the course. So you might say something like 'Go *over* the table, *under* the mat and *between* the chairs'. A good group game and a chance to introduce a lot of those difficult position words.

Big and little scavenger hunt

Reinforce your child's understanding of 'big' and 'little' with this game. Read him a list of items to find, such as socks, spoons and cups for playing indoors and leaves, stones and sticks for outdoors. He then has to find two of each item – one big and one little.

Visual skills

Your three- to four-year-old should be able to:

- match colours;
- match simple shapes;
- pick up very small items (pin-sized) with each eye covered separately;
- spot the difference between two pictures where one has a fairly obvious omission;
- match some letters such as 'v', 'o' and 'x'.

Looking games

Hunt the thimble

It does not have to be a thimble, of course; looking for a strawberry or plum might be more rewarding. This is a good group game and teaches children to look more carefully. Hide the item somewhere in the room but tell your child when she is getting 'warmer' or 'colder'.

What's the difference?

Draw two pictures but make one slightly different from the other. You could, perhaps, draw two faces but leave an ear off one; or two houses but only one with a chimney. Now see if your child can spot the difference.

What's new?

How observant is your child? Change a piece of furniture round in her bedroom or add something new and see if she can tell you what has changed.

Match it

Use two sets of ordinary playing cards for this matching game but do not use the whole set to start with. Use them for a simple matching activity by asking your child to find two the same. He will need to look at shape, number and colour to be successful at this. Later, you could turn this into a pairs game by choosing five matching pairs from the cards and turning them upside down on the table. Now take turns to turn two over at a time in an effort to find two the same.

Spot the duck

You can buy various story books which have the added interest of looking for a hidden animal on each page. However, you can incorporate this activity into any book by deciding to look out for a particular item. You might decide to spot what colour shoes everyone is wearing or perhaps see how many people in each picture look happy and how many look sad.

Play

Your three- to four-year-old should be able to:

- play co-operatively alongside and sometimes with other children;
- pretend to be something or someone else;
- use dolls, teddies or miniature people for creative, pretend play;
- pretend that a miscellaneous item such as a cardboard box is something else;
- make discoveries through experimental play.

Playtime

Box magic

Tell your child that every time you wave your magic wand, his large, cardboard box will turn into something else — but let him decide exactly what. Make it even more fun by inviting a couple of friends round and giving them a box each. The boxes can then be used together to become a variety of things from a train to a snail family's shells.

Dressing up

Never throw your old clothes, old sheets or any old material away. You will soon accumulate a useful box of dressing-up clothes. Your child will be far more inventive with these than with bought fancy-dress outfits. Your child and her friends can use masks or face paints to enhance the costumes and act out a story.

Water and sand play

Give your child a bowl of water, a bowl of wet sand, a bowl of dry sand and a variety of bottles, sieves, funnels and floating objects. She will discover all sorts of things about the properties of sand and water and about quantity and size just by playing and having fun.

Also try putting different amounts of water into jars and give your child some utensils to hit them with. She should be able to make a variety of sounds depending on the amount of water and what she hits the jars with.

Teddies' tea party

Your child can make different coloured drinks for his dolls and teddies using water and food colouring. Add washing-up liquid to make some of it bubbly. Then he can make food out of play-dough or Plasticine. He could even invent some presents and party games for the teddies. A good game to stretch the imagination.

Picture charades

Cut out pictures of animals and people (such as doctors and policemen and women) from magazines and stick them on to individual pieces of card. Take it in turns to take a card and then do a mime of that person or animal for everyone else to guess.

Age guides

Children develop at their own pace and the suggestions for what your three- to four-year-old should be doing are only averages. Some children will talk earlier than others for example, while others will be riding a two-wheeler before some children have mastered a tricycle. Many changes will take place both during this year and during the run up to school. Just make sure you encourage your child in all areas, perhaps paying particular attention to his weaknesses but without pushing him. All these activities should be fun for both of you and when you stop enjoying it, stop the activity and try again another day.

Growing in the right direction – parents' questions

> My four-year-old does not know his colours. How do I teach him?

Most children will know at least the primary colours when they start school but there are usually a few who do not. Colour awareness is therefore part of the work done by the infant teachers in the early stages. Most pre-school playgroups and nurseries also tackle colours in play situations.

However, there are plenty of activities to do at home, remembering to go at your child's pace and keep it fun. Firstly, your child needs to match colours and you can encourage this by getting him to sort coloured drinking straws into groups or by making a colour lotto game (small coloured squares which go on to a board of matching squares). Just start with red, blue, green and yellow and introduce others when your child is confident with these. Make a giant die out of a cardboard box and paint a different colour on each side. Throw the dice and then get your child to find something in the room of that colour.

Do not worry about getting him to name the colours yet but make sure you say them yourself so that he is learning as you play. Talk about colours as you are going about your daily routine, naming the colours of everyday objects such as his toothbrush or cup. Once your child is good at colour matching, see if he can find something of a particular colour in response to the word, i.e. 'Find something red' or 'Find your blue sock', correcting him gently as you go along. Start with just two colours and add another when you have some success with the first two.

> ❛ My child is not very interested in any sitting-down games although she is an expert on her bike and climbing frame. ❜

When your child starts school, she will need to have had experience of sitting down and completing a task. Perhaps you could use her outdoor interests as a starting point. She could cut out pictures from a garden toy or bicycle catalogue for instance, or else you could draw bikes and she could draw the people on them.

To help her with manipulative skills, see if she can tie some flags (which she has coloured in) on to the climbing frame, or woolly pom-poms (again made by her with your help) on to her handle bars. Choose stories about the activities which interest her and stick written labels on to her outdoor toys to introduce an interest in reading. Do not discourage her motor skills though – in fact she may enjoy joining a pre-school gymnastic club such as Tumble

Tots or Fit Kid (see the address list at the back of the book) to build on her physical skills.

(My three-year-old sometimes stammers. Should I tell him to slow down?)

No. This is quite a normal stage which many children go through, often at a time when they suddenly have a lot more to say. If you tell him to slow down, take a breath or stop and start again, then you are drawing a lot of attention to it which could make your child very aware and self-conscious. Instead, ignore it but make a point of paying more attention to *what* he is saying rather than *how* he is saying it. Give your child plenty of time to speak and slow your own speech down to a relaxed pace. Your child will pick up and respond to your anxiety so do not worry – after all it *is* only a stage which your child is going through. If it does start to worry him, then ask your health visitor or GP to refer you to a speech and language therapist for further advice.

(My three-and-a-half-year-old is very clumsy, always walking in to things and falling over. Is this normal?)

Many three- and four-year-olds seem to go through a clumsy stage as they attempt more difficult tasks such as going further up the climbing frame or reaching high speeds on their trikes. Control of her body will still be developing so some scrapes and bruises are inevitable. Try and encourage your child to stop and think before she moves. You could try setting up an obstacle course and then get your child actually to stop and say what she is going to do before she starts. Get your child to do activities which require more care and balance, such as walking along planks or running in and out of obstacles. If your child seems to move awkwardly and if her walking or running looks immature, ask your health visitor to refer you to a paediatrician for further advice.

❝ *I can't always understand my three-year-old although he's got plenty to say for himself. Will he grow out of it?* ❞

By three, your child should be intelligible although he may still leave 's-' off the beginning of words like '(s)pider' and '(s)tamp'. He may also substitute 't' and 'd' for 'k' and 'g' so that 'gate' is pronounced as 'date' and 'key' as 'tea'. Other immaturities may involve 'l', 'sh', 'th' and 'r' which may not be correct until he is four or five. If your child is still not using 'k', 'g', or 's' blends by three-and-a-half or if he has problems with other sounds, then ask your GP or health visitor to refer you to a speech and language therapist for further advice.

CHAPTER THREE

One year to go – getting your four- to five-year-old ready

Before you know what has happened, your child will only have one year to go before one of the biggest milestones of his life – starting school. While you pause for breath, wondering where the last four years have gone, you may have a sudden feeling of panic. Thoughts like 'Will he *really* be ready?', 'He's only a baby' or 'But he doesn't know how to . . .' will immediately come to mind. However, you will see some quite dramatic maturation during this final pre-school year and your clumsy four-year-old struggling to get into his shorts and hiding behind you whenever anyone speaks to him will suddenly blossom into a mature and independent child looking forward to school with heaps of confidence. Especially if you take the time to prepare him well.

In this chapter, we will see how movement, manipulation, communication, understanding, visual skills and play will develop during this year and how to help your child with that development. He may also be ready to tackle some pre-reading, pre-writing and Maths games, which are outlined in chapter 10.

Remember that children develop at their own rates and the age range (four to five years) given for managing these tasks is only a rough guideline. And, of course, because children start school at different ages, 'one year to go' may mean three-and-a-half to four-and-a-half years rather than four to five years, which will obviously lead to wider variations in attainment.

While carrying out activities, particularly in the play section, a good balance needs to be made between playing with your child and allowing him to have time and space to experiment and develop on his own. You will gradually become aware of when to intervene and when to step back and let your child have control of the activity.

Physical development and movement

Your four- to five-year-old should be able to:

- walk and run up and down stairs, one foot to a step;
- climb an easy tree;
- walk and run on tiptoe;
- hop;
- stand on one leg while you count to ten;
- sit cross-legged;
- hit a ball with a bat (though not very accurately);
- go up and down a ladder easily;
- walk along a line;
- use a spade effectively for digging a hole.

Move it games

Hop-painting

Fill up a deep tray or old washing-up bowl with thick paint. Get your child to take her shoes and socks off, stand in the paint and then walk, run or hop all over a large sheet of paper to make patterns. To encourage hopping or balancing, you could get your child to use just one foot for painting, but let her wear a wellington on the other foot – she is bound to topple over and get paint on it!

Newspaper cricket

An ideal way to get your child to hit a ball with a bat, especially as it can be played indoors too. In this game the bat is a rolled up newspaper and the ball a single sheet of paper, screwed up.

Or cut fish shapes out of the newspaper and use the newspaper bat to bang on the floor behind them. Once the technique is perfected, this will make the fish move along the floor. Make it a race to see who can get their fish across the room first without touching them with anything.

Paint can stilts

An excellent way to help your child with balance and co-ordination. Take two old paint cans or large baby milk cans and attach cord or rope to each can. The cans are upside down so that your child can put one foot on each. One end of the cord is attached to one side of the can, the other end to the other side. The cord should be long enough for your child to hold while standing on the cans. Now see if he can walk along without falling off.

Hop-scotch

The old game of hopping quickly along a sequence of numbered squares while kicking a stone can be adapted to suit your child's level of ability. If your child is not familiar with numbers, work out a sequence of colours. Or put some hoops out and see if your child can hop from one to another.

Skipping games

The easiest form of skipping is to get one person to hold each end of a rope. Then see if your child can jump over it with her feet together. Now swing the rope back and forth gently and see if she can jump over it and back again while you do so. Try saying a rhyme while you do this activity to encourage your child to skip to a rhythm. Eventually, you can swing the rope right over her head and see if she can jump over the rope when it gets to her feet – very hard for a pre-schooler.

Manipulation

Your four- to five-year-old should be able to:

- thread small beads to make a necklace, using a large needle and thread (he will not be able to thread the needle);
- build a tower of more than ten bricks;
- draw a recognisable person, and usually a house;
- cut more accurately with scissors;
- do neat colouring, keeping within the lines;
- do large buttons up;
- pour juice out of a jug into a cup;
- trace a picture;
- unscrew the top of a bottle or jar;
- use a fork and spoon together.

Finger games

Box it

Collect together a selection of jars, bottles, boxes and other containers with different tops. Hide a crisp, raisin or sweet in one of them and see how quickly your child can find the treasure. A good incentive to try those difficult lids.

Cake decoration

Make fairy cakes together (or perhaps a larger sponge cake), ice them and then let your child have a free hand at the decorating. Collect together small items to stick on the cakes — silver balls, raisins, hundreds and thousands, smarties and so on. Let her make patterns with the decorations. This is a good activity to help manipulation.

Message in a bottle

Take turns to hide something in the house, then draw a clue on a piece of paper and put it in a plastic bottle. So, for example, if you hid the treasure under the table, you could draw the table on a piece of paper, roll it up and put it in the bottle. Your child has to get the paper out of the bottle (not always easy) and guess from the drawing where the treasure is. Suggest to your child that she chooses fairly easy things to draw when she has her turn.

Tricky pass the parcel

Play the popular party game of pass the parcel: your family or a group of children sits in a circle and passes the parcel from one to the other until the music stops, then whoever has the parcel has to take a layer of wrapping off. Make the layers of wrapping more difficult to undo by tying string tightly round with bows.

Cut it

Encourage your child to practise cutting using safe round-ended child scissors. One easy activity with a very pleasing result is to fold a large, thin piece of paper in half and then in half again. Get your child to snip round the edge, cut the corners off and, if she can manage it, cut small shapes into the edge of the paper. Even if her cutting is haphazard, when she opens it out, she will have made an interesting pattern.

Communication

Your four- to five-year-old should be able to:

- use sentences of four to six words, often longer;
- use his large vocabulary of several thousand words;
- use grammatical sentences with mistakes becoming fewer;
- give more detailed accounts of what he has been doing in your absence;
- make himself understood to anyone who listens;
- ask endless questions;
- recite and sing nursery rhymes;
- join in with family conversations;
- tell familiar stories and sometimes make up his own;
- answer the telephone coherently.

Talking games

Story turns

Make up a story as you go along to stretch your child's communication skills and imagination. You start with an interesting situation such as 'I was walking along the road when something strange popped out of a hole' then see if your child can add a bit more. Keep taking turns to tell a bit of the story until it is finished. Your child will find this difficult to start with but practice will turn this into a very enjoyable and rewarding activity.

Tiger hunt

Another game to help the imagination as well as stretch your child's memory. You start by saying 'When we went on a tiger hunt, we went through some tall grass'. Then your child repeats this and adds something else such as 'We went through some tall grass and then across a muddy field'. Make it easier to remember by adding actions and noises. Once you find the tiger, you can run back home by remembering the sequence in reverse order – quite hard without you doing the actions as clues.

Snap for a reason

Try this with your five-year-old but if she finds it hard, leave it for six months and try again. Use ordinary picture snap games but make it more interesting by adding some cards of your own, made out of magazine pictures stuck onto card. Now play snap but instead of saying 'snap' if both cards are identical, say 'snap' if they have something in common – perhaps they are both animals or both have wheels. Any reason counts so long as it is explained properly by you or your child.

If I was . . .

Start by saying 'If I was as small as a button, my bed would be a match box' and see if your child can think of anything else – what would her house, chair or cup be for example? What would she eat or drink? When you run out of ideas, try 'If I was as big as a tree' and imagine what life would be like then.

Guess who I am

Help your child think of questions to ask for this game or indeed any other version of twenty questions. Restrict it so that you either choose to be something in the room, someone you know or somebody you watch on television. It is best if your child chooses something or somebody first so that you can demonstrate useful questions such as 'Is it a man?', 'Does he live near here?' or 'Is he older than you?'. Now let your child have a go at asking.

Understanding

Your four- to five-year-old should be able to:

- understand most of what is said to him;
- ask when he does not understand;
- understand 'Why?' questions, although his reasons may seem illogical;
- laugh at funny stories and nonsense words;
- understand the simple rules of a game;
- understand about telling the time, sometimes relating a particular time to meal times or bed time;
- understand what two adults are talking about when he listens in (so be careful what you say!);
- understand a story with a moral ending;
- follow longer and more complex instructions during play;
- listen carefully to what others are saying to him.

Games for understanding

Listen and draw

Give your child very precise instructions for drawing a picture, bit by bit at first and then all in one go to make it more difficult. For example, you could say 'Draw a circle with a dot in the middle, then draw two banana shapes joined on to the circle, one each side. Then do a little line, a finger gap under the dot'. If he remembers this, all he has to do is add the eyes and he should have a face. You could do a copy of the picture first so that he can check how near he was at the end.

Maps

Make a giant road map of a pretend town together on a large piece of paper, drawing in lots of landmarks such as trees, shops, post boxes and car parks. Now give your child a toy car and instructions like 'Go up the main street and park next to the post box'.

Describe it scavenger hunt

Introduce your child to different descriptive words (adjectives) with this game. You can ask her to find something round and smooth or sharp and jagged or soft and silky. Make it as easy or difficult as you want and play indoors or outdoors.

Why oh why oh why . . . ?

Introduce your child to some logical thinking and really stretch his mind. 'Why are cars all different colours?', 'Why don't we build our houses in trees?', 'Why do we need curtains?' or 'Why do children go to school?' should start you off. Your child is probably at the stage of asking some pretty awkward questions herself so now it is your turn!

Mood charades

This is another good game for introducing descriptive words as well as a look at non-verbal communication (body language and facial expressions). You whisper to your child a mood to act out – angry, sad, happy, shy, excited and so on. His friends or the rest of the family then have to guess what mood he is in. Another version is to ask each player to walk across the room in a certain way – slowly, quickly, happily, stupidly – and again the other players guess the act.

Visual skills

Your four- to five-year-old should be able to:

- spot the difference between two complex pictures;
- build three steps out of six bricks after being shown how;
- copy 'v', 'h', 't', 'o', 'x' and sometimes 'l', 'c', 'u' and other letters (very variable);
- build a bridge out of three bricks;
- match shapes in a lotto game.

Looking games

Spot the mistake

Draw a picture for your child with a mistake in it – make it obvious at first like a man with only one ear or a house with the front door upstairs. Then make it more difficult to spot. So perhaps you could draw a more complicated picture of a house and garden but there could be a tiny cat in the garden with one eye missing, an upstairs window with only one curtain or an upside-down milk bottle on the doorstep.

Reflections

Get your child to really look in the mirror at herself. Then see if she notices how different she looks in the back of a spoon, a pool of water or a shiny metal saucepan. Hold other things up to the mirror including her name and see what they look like back to front.

Looking through the keyhole

Cut a keyhole shape in a large piece of card. Now hold the keyhole card over a picture or object so that your child can only see part of it. Can she guess what it is? If not, try showing her a selection of pictures before playing the game so she knows what to look out for. Start with a fairly big keyhole shape and gradually make it smaller.

Deliver the letters

Write a different letter of the alphabet in lower case (i.e. not in capitals) on the front of a selection of old envelopes. Pin badges with the same letters on to the front of a selection of your child's dolls and soft toys. Now see if he can deliver the right letter to the right toy by matching the letters of the alphabet together.

Home-made puzzles

Jigsaw puzzles are very good for visual skills as well as eye–hand co-ordination. As well as bought ones, you can make your own simply by cutting up old pictures and photos. Children love doing puzzles of themselves so try sticking old photos onto card and cutting them up into pieces to put back together again.

Play

Your four- to five-year-old should be able to:

- play in a group of children, taking turns and beginning to pay attention to the rules of the game;
- make pretend people or toys say and do things in an imaginative way;
- play a game for longer than ten minutes;
- discuss with other children what to play and then play it;
- make up a game, inventing rules as she goes along.

Play time

Make a board game

Get a large sheet of paper or card and draw a track of squares on it like a conventional board game. Your child can then colour some of the squares in red and decide what forfeits a player who lands on one of these squares will have. You can either write these on the squares or on to individual pieces of card which the player takes when landing on a red square. At first, your child will probably base the forfeits on other games – go back three spaces, miss a turn and so on. But encourage him to become more inventive. Perhaps the forfeit could be to sing a nursery rhyme or hop across the room, for example.

If you're happy

Sing the old favourite, 'If you're happy and you know it, clap your hands' but get your child to invent new actions to go with the song – 'If you're happy and you know it, pull your ear' perhaps. Now see if she can change the first bit and accompany the song with varied facial expressions. Start with 'If you're sad and you know it' and build up from there.

Doctors and nurses

This favourite pretence can lead to some imaginative group play. There is no need to buy any expensive equipment, just old shirts for doctors' coats and old sheets, ripped up, for bandages. Give your child a selection of empty containers and let her decide what ailments they can cure. Avoid sexual stereotypes when children are deciding what role to play.

Shopping

Take some empty containers, carrier bags and cardboard boxes and

PREPARE YOUR CHILD FOR SCHOOL

you have got a shop. Play with your child or encourage a group of children to play together. You could have a row of shops and help your child sort out the dressing-up clothes into a dress shop, the containers into a food shop and so on. One could even be a hairdresser's. Try and stand back once you have started the game off and let your child make the decisions and inventions needed for this game.

Change-the-rules tag

Start with a simple game of tag – one player is 'it' and tries to catch someone else who then becomes 'it'. Then start adding the rules such as 'If you are touching the wall, you can't be caught' or 'If you get caught, sit down until another player touches you'. Encourage your child to think of as many rules as she can and never belittle her ideas – simply try them out and she can decide if they work or not.

Growing in the right direction – parents' questions

I try to encourage my child to play imaginative games like "cooking" and "shops" but I cannot afford all the toys he needs.

Remember that using a cardboard box with the knobs drawn on for a cooker requires far more imagination than using a large realistic model. And deciding what to use as a shopping trolley, whether it is a wheelbarrow or a box with wheels drawn on, requires far more thought than having a toy trolley to hand. Children can have too many small versions of the real thing which leave little to the imagination. Try and think back to what *you* used to play with as a child – many of the toys today were not even available 30 years ago.

> *How can I improve my child's memory? It seems such an important skill for coping with school.*

There are three types of memory you might consider. Firstly there is your child's long term memory for things he has done in his life. Most of us remember very little about our lives before the age of two and your child will probably be the same. But keep the past alive and in your child's mind by referring to photographs and diaries which you can keep as a record of everything you have done.

Secondly there is short term memory for things we look at (visual memory). There are many games to help with this – try pelmanism (pairs), where you put out pairs of pictures upside down and take turns to turn two over, aiming to find a pair. You might also play Kim's game where you put some objects on a tray and remove one while your child closes her eyes. Can she remember what was there?

Thirdly, there is short term memory for things we hear (auditory memory). Try giving your child three things to remember when you go shopping or three things to fetch from upstairs. You can also try games like 'I went to market . . .' where your child has to remember an increasingly long list of items. See if your child can improve her memory of the list by closing her eyes and visualising all the things she has to remember.

> *When my child is sent to fetch something from his room, he always says "I can't find it" even if it's sitting right in front of his eyes. How can I make him more observant?*

Do not accept 'I can't find it' as an answer. Go with him and instead of finding it for him, tell him it is there (so he does not give up) and if necessary give him hints or tell him when he is getting warm.

PREPARE YOUR CHILD FOR SCHOOL

It may also be that he just is not interested in finding his jumper or lost shoe. So play hunt the treasure by hiding something worth finding, such as a favourite snack, in the room. Play some of the looking games in this chapter as well as old standards like hide and seek. Children do get more observant as their concentration improves, which often happens once they start school.

(*My child is so bossy! Whenever she's playing with friends, it's always her doing the organising and deciding what to play.*)

By four, most children have very established personalities and it could be that your child is just a born leader – something to be proud of. Accept her personality as it is but at the same time give her some opportunities to take a more passive role, especially if she looks set to boss the teacher about! Give her the chance to play with older children where she may be less inclined to take the lead all the time. Teach her to take turns in deciding what to play, without criticising her as you will not want to curb her natural confidence. You need to intervene at first by saying to your child 'Have you asked Tracey what she wants to do?'. You could even make up a story about a bossy girl who forgot to ask other children what they wanted to play – your child will probably think he is awful!

(*My child never attempts anything difficult. When we go to the adventure playground, for instance, he only tries the equipment he knows he can do.*)

Give your child plenty of praise for the things he *can* do to boost his confidence. See if you can make those things slightly more difficult so, for example, get him to go down the slide in different, more daring ways. Or if he can balance well on the beam, see if he can do it backwards. Never force your child to try something he does not want to. See if he will do it with you to start with. If the slide seems a little too high, go up with him but give the minimal help needed, pointing out afterwards how little you helped him, if at all. The same principles apply to anything else he is learning, whether it is recognising letters or dressing himself. Always praise what he can do and build on that in very gradual stages.

CHAPTER FOUR

Helping your child with goodbyes

Ideally, as you say goodbye to your child on his first day, he will say a cheery 'goodbye' back to you and eagerly start school, barely giving you another thought. No tears, no fuss, no tantrums – from you or your child! However, if your child is clingy or shy and finds separation from you hard to bear, you may wonder how either of you is going to cope.

Helping your child say goodbye starts from a much earlier age of course. And during the pre-school years, it is a rare child who does not have the occasional clingy phase or at the very least, the odd time when he wants Mum or Dad and nobody else will do. If these stages are tackled sensibly, your child will soon learn that you do come back and will then feel far more secure when he is left. A group of children starting school for the first time will all have had different experiences. Some will have working parents with frequent separation as a way of life while others will have spent much more time at home. Whatever the home circumstances, by the first day at school, your child should have:

- spent time away from you regularly – at least two three-hour sessions a week, preferably at a pre-school group;

- spent time away from you in the care of at least three different adults; maybe friends, child-minders, grandparents or play-group leaders;
- spent the equivalent of a school day, including a meal, away from you.

And it's goodbye from you . . .

Be careful not to fall into the trap of wanting your child to need you, and only you. Of course, it is lovely to be wanted and needed so much, but having a child who is independent and confident with other people does not mean she does not still need and love her parents. It can be quite disheartening when your child runs into playgroup so eagerly that she forgets to say goodbye at all. And it is difficult to feel pleased when you go to collect her only to hear her mutter, 'Wait a minute, I'll just finish this'. You should, of course, feel pleased that your child is becoming so independent. But there will always be part of you which really quite enjoys the child who needs you, who rushes over as soon as you return and who expresses just a little regret at your departing. So take some time to look at your own feelings and take note of the following:

- Your child will pick up on your feelings, whether they are of anxiety or just a need to give your child one more hug. Feel confident and positive yourself and you will help your child feel the same.
- Always remind yourself that you really *do* want an independent and confident child. You will not be helping her at all if you do not give her the opportunity to separate from you at an early age.
- Remind yourself that your child gains a lot from relating to other adults and being part of a group of children.

PREPARE YOUR CHILD FOR SCHOOL

- Having time away from your child is good for you too. Parents need time on their own and temper tantrums are ever so much easier to deal with after a break.
- Do not fall into the trap of thinking that your child is *always* better off with you.

When to start the goodbyes

This will depend a lot on your circumstances. Parents returning to work early will, in many ways, find saying goodbye a lot easier, or at least the baby will. Babies under nine months rarely mind at all when you leave them and some will go straight through to school with few problems. Others will go through clingy phases, particularly if they spent longer at home during the early years, although a lot will also depend on personality. Clinginess, shyness or tantrums when you leave will be dealt with differently depending on the age of your child. Just remember not to leave saying goodbye too late. Your child will need plenty of experience at being apart from you before school starts.

Nought to three months

Your baby will already have built up a close relationship with you, recognising and reacting to the sound of your voice. However, she will not yet have developed a fear of strangers or separation. She will be quite happy to be left with someone else so long as she is fed, can sleep and is kept comfortable. This is a good time, therefore, to start going out with your partner occasionally. She will not yet be learning about coping without you – she will hardly notice that you have gone – but it will set a trend for later on. At this stage, it is *you* who needs to get used to leaving *her*.

Three to nine months

Your baby will form a much closer attachment to you during this stage and may even object when you leave the room. However, she will be easily distracted and will usually form other relationships with ease. This is a good time, therefore, to choose a minder or nanny if you are returning to work. Your baby should settle in well and if you continue working until school age, your child should start school with a great deal of independence and probably confidence. If you are staying at home with your child, have friends round and make sure that your baby at least gets used to you leaving the room.

Nine to 18 months

This is the stage when some babies develop a fear of strangers although your child will probably separate from you well if it is with a familiar adult. Try to use carers and babysitters who are known to your child and if she does object to being left, still go of course, but work out a regime which makes parting easier for both of you. She will have no sense of time so 'Be back soon' or 'I won't be a minute' are meaningless. It is usually best at this stage to keep explanations and goodbyes short and simple. If you are staying at home with your child, try joining a mother and toddler group or having groups of children and parents round to play. Your child will get used to other adults as well as other children and will probably venture further away from you, secure in the knowledge that you are still there.

One-and-a-half to three

This is often a clingy age, particularly for children who are not used to being left. You may find that your child objects noisily at the moment of separation but settles down quickly once you have gone. You could ask the minder how long it takes your child to settle, or you could even listen outside the door for a while to reassure yourself. Your child will now understand simple explanations so you can give her an idea of when you are coming back. He will not have a concept of time yet but you could say something like 'I'll be back once you've played and had your dinner' or 'I'm going to the shops and to post some letters and then I'll be back to collect you'.

Three to five years

These are the years for joining a pre-school playgroup or nursery. Again, many children react when you say goodbye but settle in quickly once you have gone. However, most children get into a routine quickly and remember that you always come back at the end of the session. Your child will be communicating more efficiently now and you can discuss what is going to happen in advance. She can also tell you about her thoughts and feelings. You will probably adopt a goodbye regime which best suits your child – some children like to be left with the minimum of fuss, some like you to linger for a while and others will need plenty of hugs and kisses as you depart.

Five years and over

School should not be the first separation from you and there should be few problems if your child is well prepared. However, if your child is anxious about school, this may manifest itself in clingy behaviour. Your child will start to see things from your point of view now, appreciating that you need to work or want to have a night out with your partner. Confident children may be ready for overnight or weekend visits to friends or relatives. However, if this is a new idea to your child, do not introduce it at the same time as she is settling into school. Most children need to tackle one new event at a time.

How to say goodbye

Should you use the long lingering farewell or make a dash for the door? Should you give your child long explanations, or not tell her that you are going until the very last minute? There are different ways of saying goodbye and different techniques to settle your child in with someone new. The goodbye routine which you adopt will largely depend on the age and personality of the child. The most important thing is to be consistent. Most pre-school children and, indeed, those just starting school, respond well to a routine. If you normally kiss her goodbye but then one day rush off in a hurry with barely a 'cheerio', this could upset a normally calm and cheery child. Similarly, you need to ensure that you are not late, do not forget an essential piece of equipment such as a toy, coat or lunch box and stick fairly rigidly to the routine which you have adopted. If you establish a good, workable routine but then one day, your child clings to your leg for no apparent reason, do not automatically change your routine. Stick to the same goodbye sequence but, at the same time, try to find out if anything is upsetting your child. At the beginning though, you may need to find the best technique for saying goodbye more or less by trial and error. You will soon find out if saying a while to settle her in soothes or upsets your child. And you will quickly find out if your child needs a familiar toy or, if in fact, this just leads to squabbles with other children. Try the following goodbye routines and see what suits you both.

The quick get-away

It is never a good idea just to disappear without warning, even with a very young child. It may work at first but he will soon start objecting once you have gone. You may then find he becomes clingy all the time for fear that you will suddenly go. It may be better to give your child a warning even if it is a very quick, last minute one, giving her little chance to react badly. The quick get-away is particularly suitable for younger children. Just a quick 'Bye-bye, Barbara will look after you until we're back' followed by a sharp exit is fine. You may still be leaving while your child is crying or shouting his objections but that is probably better than hanging around while the objections get louder and stronger. You will, of course, want reassurance that your child does settle once you have gone.

The settle-in-slowly routine

This can be suitable for a three- to four-year-old child starting at a pre-school group, particularly if she has only had infrequent separation from you before. You may want a very slow settle-in routine whereby you spend one or two sessions at the group with your child before leaving her at all. After that you could just leave for part of the session until your child is ready to stay on her own for the full time. This will not work well if your child spends all the time right next to you to ensure that you are not about to leave. You also need to check the policy of the group before your child starts. Some groups encourage Mums and Dads to stay and settle their child in while others may need some persuasion.

The bribery scheme

Your child may need an added incentive to separate from you. However, be careful not to set a routine of real bribery where your child expects sweets or a present every time you leave him for more than ten minutes. On the other hand, if you plan something for your child to look forward to after you get back from work, this can sometimes help. It will certainly reassure him that you are definitely coming back. The treat could be a trip to the park or a drink in a café but remember that your child may be particularly tired if he has just started nursery or playgroup. An ice-cream or a cuddle together with a new library book may be better than an action-packed afternoon or evening.

If you feel that your child is trying it on with tantrums as you leave, you can try a star chart. Every time your child goes into nursery or school without a fuss, give him a star with a treat once he has won a certain number of stars. Do not, however, try this if your child is genuinely having difficulty settling in. The extra pressure of trying to win a star by doing something which is quite beyond him will not help at all.

The take-a-toy ploy

This can help, but needs to be thought out very carefully first. For a start, some playgroups and nurseries actively discourage it because toys tend to get lost or cause problems with sharing. On the other hand, if your child is one of just a few children at a child-minder's, taking a familiar toy can help your child during the settling-in period. It is worth discussing it all first with the minder or group leader – bearing in mind that the familiar toy will only be used while the child still feels unsettled. This may be for a few days or a few weeks and may just be needed for the first few minutes of each session when it can then be put away safely. On a practical note, if the toy is particularly precious, you might try to get a duplicate one for home just in case of loss or damage.

Dummies and blankets may be helpful for under-twos and could be handed over to the minder to use at sleep or rest times only. After two, such comforters are probably best discouraged unless the child still has a sleep time.

Some children may be helped by having something new to take along on the first day – perhaps a new flask, lunch box or woolly hat for play-time (all named of course). This applies to the first day at school as well.

The send-someone-else-in routine

It may be that you are the worst person to take your child to nursery or playgroup. Perhaps you are finding it difficult yourself or maybe your child is responding to your anxiety. Maybe your child plays you up but is perfectly all right when your partner or a friend takes her. If you do try this, make sure that your child is happy with the arrangement and that you get positive feedback from the group that she is settling in well.

How to say hello

Saying hello again is always a moment to look forward to whether it is after the first day at school or after you have been out shopping for half an hour. This should be the easiest part of the separation process but children can take us by surprise, not always reacting in the way we expect.

The big hello

This is one of the best reactions from your point of view. Your child is busy but when he sees you, greets you with a smile or runs towards you eagerly. You will know immediately that he has been happy in your absence but you will also know that he is pleased to see you again. It is always reassuring if you see your child before he sees you especially when he is happily engrossed in something.

The wait-I'm-busy hello

Your child may show that he is pleased to see you with a smile but does not rush over to greet you as he just cannot tear himself away from the toys. You may be eager for a hug but remember that this is a sure sign that he is completely settled in the environment, secure in the knowledge that you have returned as promised. Never show disappointment that you did not get 'the big hello' but show your own pleasure in seeing him.

The big ignore

Your child may ignore you completely, carrying on with what she is doing without seeming to notice your arrival at all. This may be her way of punishing you for leaving without her. Just make sure that *you* show your pleasure at seeing her again and after a few minutes, you will get the greeting you deserve. Be careful not to start chatting to other parents or teachers while she is carrying out 'the big ignore'. Make yourself available for the hello when it comes.

The gush of tears

Your child may seem perfectly happy until he sees you at which point he just bursts into tears. This is a common reaction from a child who is still in the process of settling in. He is overwhelmed with relief at your return and cannot express it any other way.

Shy or clingy – parents' questions

❝ Whenever I take my child to play at a friend's house, he becomes very shy and won't leave my side. He's not normally like this and I think he's putting it on. What should I do? **❞**

Only a very few children act shyly on purpose. If your child does seem to be acting then it is probably to gain your attention. If you think he is acting, try ignoring it but reward him with your full attention whenever he goes to play with others without a fuss. However, it is more likely that your child just finds certain situations difficult to deal with or even frightening. Never force your child to play with others on his own. Try instead to build up his confidence by gradually working towards that objective. Start by inviting friends round to play with your child in his own environment. Then go with him when he is invited to play with other children but once he is settled, leave for part of the time. Gradually increase the length of your absence until he feels confident enough to go and play on his own. He will need a lot of encouragement so do not belittle his fears, make excuses for him or draw attention to his shyness in front of other people. Do not be tempted to avoid difficult situations altogether. It will not help your child's shyness if he never has the opportunity to go and play with other children, even if this seems to be the easiest policy in the short term.

> *My shy daughter will be starting school next term and I'm worried about how she'll cope in class. Should I mention this to the teacher?*

That might be a good idea as it helps the teacher to have as much information as possible about each child. It may also help you feel less anxious if the school is informed. However, do not worry too much as your daughter certainly will not be the only shy child in the class and the teacher will be experienced at helping all types of children to settle in.

In the meantime, start helping her develop the confidence to cope with new situations. Make a point of praising her and listening to her so that she develops a high sense of self-esteem. At the same time, give her plenty of experience of mixing with other children and talking to different adults, encouraging and reinforcing all her efforts. Talk about what is going to happen, perhaps using books from the library, and make sure that she has visited the school and met some of the other children. Remind yourself that being shy need only be a temporary phase – most children develop self-confidence with help and encouragement. So never criticise her for being shy, accept her personality as it is but give her the help she needs. Remember, as well, that many children are very different at school than at home. Many is the parent who has chatted to the teacher about their child only to come away wondering if they were talking about the same person!

> *I remember clinging to my mother and screaming on my first day at school. My daughter is just like me and I'm worried that it will be the same for her.*

Even though some aspects of our personality are inherited, do not assume that your child will be shy or clingy just because you were. You must also bear in mind that circumstances have changed: schools now are much more aware of the need for school preparation. More children have some pre-school experience in a nursery or playgroup and so starting school is not such an enormous step. Make sure that your child is prepared for school both by having experience at a pre-school group and by knowing what to expect when she gets there. Ensure that you are prepared as well. You will need to put your own experience to one side and feel positive that your child will settle more quickly. After all, sensing your anxiety will certainly not help her feel confident about starting.

My four-year-old chats away confidently at home but never says a word to anyone when we're out. He enjoys playgroup but doesn't seem to mix very well. How will he cope at school if he won't talk to the teacher or the children?

Start by reinforcing his confidence about speaking at home. Show an interest in everything he says, particularly when it is in front of or to visitors. Never pressurise him into speaking when you are out – if he feels that he has to perform then he is more likely to clam up. Casually try to include your child in the conversation without expecting him to join in unless he really wants to. For instance, you could say 'We went swimming today, didn't we?' which he can respond to if and when he is ready. Beware of reprimanding him too much for interrupting or shouting as he will not yet have all the social graces of adult conversation. When he is ready, show him how rewarding talking can be – getting him to ask the shop assistants for his favourite food, for example. If he is happy at playgroup, then do not worry too much if he is still very much on the sidelines. Ask the playgroup leader if he gets on with any particular child so that you can invite him round to your home. A one-to-one relationship may be easier for your child to start with.

PREPARE YOUR CHILD FOR SCHOOL

(How do I say goodbye on the first day at school?)

Make sure that your child knows exactly what is going to happen. You will very likely be asked to take your child into the classroom where he will be met by the teacher whom he has probably already met. If you know of another child starting school, try going in together as it may be easier to say goodbye to two friends. Do not arrive too early and have to hang around, or too late so that you feel rushed. Say goodbye in the same way as you always have done and then leave. Do not hover anxiously and do not go back into the room once you have left. If he seems upset or unduly anxious, you can always telephone the school during the morning to check that he did then settle in well.

CHAPTER FIVE

Help yourself – steps to independence

When your child starts school, she will not be able to take you along to help her with all those daily tasks – whether it is turning on the tap, opening her lunch box or getting her coat on and off. Of course, the teacher will be there to help but she will not expect, or be able, to wash the hands of twenty or thirty children or dress them all individually for gym! That does not mean that she will expect all new entrants to do everything for themselves. The teacher will be used to helping with shoe laces, awkward fasteners and the like and will be encouraging your child to become even more independent, particularly during the first couple of terms.

You can help in two ways. Firstly, you can encourage your child to do more things for herself especially during the year before school entry. And secondly, you can ensure that she goes to school with fasteners and shoes which she can cope with. Obviously being independent also involves being confident while you are not there and this is dealt with in chapter 4 (Helping your child with good-byes). The more your child can do for herself, the more confidently she will set off for school, so start by helping her tackle the following tricky tasks.

Ten tricky tasks

Tricky task no. 1 – getting dressed and undressed

Getting undressed is the easiest part of this task and many children can get loose clothing and socks off before they are two. While your child is in the process of learning to dress, give him easy clothes such as track suits, or shorts and T-shirts so that he is successful early on. You will still need to help with buttons and zips to start with but give your child confidence by choosing clothes with few fasteners, and shoes or trainers with velcro straps. Put all *your* old clothes into a dressing-up box so that your child is practising the art of dressing and undressing without even realising it. Practise fastenings by dressing dolls and teddies – you can even buy learn-to-dress dolls and clowns designed specifically for this purpose.

Give your child plenty of time to dress and when he gets stuck, *show* him how to tackle a particular garment rather than doing it for him. Let your child have some say in the clothes he wears – this will ensure that he *wants* to get them on, which is half the battle won. You could even change the buttons to bright shiny ones or ones in his favourite colour so that he is more likely to have a go at them. Attach a key-ring to a zip as this makes it easier to pull up and down; and teach your child that labels go on the inside of a garment. You could even put a badge or sticker on the front of a T-shirt or jumper to help your child get it on the right way round. And if it *does* end up on back to front and his socks on inside out, leave them exactly as they are and praise your child's efforts. By the time your child starts school, he should be able to dress and undress independently for gym – but do not be surprised if he comes home looking more like an extra from *Oliver* than the neat child you sent out in the morning.

Tricky task no. 2 – doing up shoes

Everyday shoes need to be sturdy with a good fastening but slippers, slip-on canvas shoes and boots will give your child some independence. If your child is confused with left and right, just ask her to choose her favourite foot – you could even give it a name – then mark that shoe so that she always gets the right shoe on the right foot. Alternatively, put different coloured socks on your child which match stickers on the appropriate shoe or else put stickers on the outward-facing side of each shoe and teach your child to keep the stickers facing outwards. Velcro fastenings are ideal and buckles are easier than lace-ups. With buckles, show your child how to pull the strap through tightly, marking the correct hole with a coloured pen. However, sooner or later your child will certainly acquire lace-ups and she can start practising the necessary manipulative skills now. Practise threading, gluing pieces of string on to paper to make snake patterns and putting ribbons into her doll's hair. When you think she is ready, show her how to tie a bow, one step at a time. Firstly just practise the single knot, then how to bend one lace in half and so on. Do not sit opposite your child when you demonstrate – this will only confuse – sit her next to you or on your lap so that she sees it from the right angle. Explanations are easiest if you colour or mark half of each shoe lace so that the two ends are different colours.

Tricky task no. 3 – putting on coats and gloves

By school age, your child should be able to get his coat on and off and do the buttons and zip up. Do not worry if he still needs some help with the fastenings, but make it easier by putting on different coloured buttons and sewing matching thread around the corresponding button hole. Mittens are easier than gloves but if your child does have gloves, he may need plenty of practice before he starts school. Teach him to spread his fingers out as widely as possible as he puts them on. Gloves tend to get lost so it may be worth attaching them to the sleeves or hanging a long string attaching both together which runs up one sleeve, along his back, and down the other sleeve.

Tricky task no. 4 – recognising possessions

Start writing your child's name on her possessions well before she starts school. If she sees it constantly on her bedroom door, in her books or on her cup, then by school age she may well be able to identify her possessions by the name tape only. Buy name tapes in clear, lower case print (i.e. not capitals) or write her name in the same way. To start with, you can make it easier by sewing picture emblems on to garments and putting stickers on to lunch boxes. To help her recognise her name, write out the names of all the family on to individual cards. Have two for each name and then play snap or pairs. Write the names in different colours to start with and then write just the first letter of each name in a different colour. Eventually, she will be able to pick her own name out without the colour clues.

Tricky task no. 5 – using the toilet

By the time your child starts school, he should be able to use the toilet independently and wash his hands afterwards. This should be no problem provided you have not continued to help your child long after it is necessary, simply because it is easier or to avoid any spills. Your child may have needed nagging to ensure that he flushes the toilet and washes his hands every time. Nagging does eventually pay off and by school age, this should be more or less automatic. Teach your son to stand up at the toilet and wipe his penis after-wards. Girls should be taught to wipe from front to back to avoid the spread of infection. Children in a hurry tend to just wave their hands at the water so encourage the use of soap by choosing some in a favourite colour or perhaps in the shape of an animal.

Tricky task no. 6 – blowing noses

This is a very important skill as keeping a nose well blown helps to guard against infection spreading to other parts, causing blocked ears and temporary deafness. Your child should have a tissue or hanky with her whenever she has a cold or runny nose and should use it (rather than her sleeve) automatically. If your child can wipe her nose but finds the blowing action difficult, play blowing games with her when she has not got a cold. Hold a flat piece of card horizontally in front of your child's face, with one end just under her nose. Place a ball of tissue paper on top and see if she can blow it off with air from her nose. Or hold a mirror in the same way for her to steam up. Now try blow-football using air through noses only. Or hold a mouth organ or similar noise-maker against her nose to see if she can make a noise with it. Remind your child to keep her mouth shut when she blows and to throw the tissue into the bin straight afterwards. Encourage her by buying her a named hanky or some brightly-coloured tissues.

Tricky task no. 7 – eating dinner

If your child is going to have school dinners, he will need to be able to use a knife and fork effectively. And if he is going to have packed lunches, you will need to ensure that he can open and close his box and flask. If he finds pouring difficult and is likely to come home looking like he has fallen into the swimming pool, give him a flask with a straw rather than with a cup.

At home, make sure your child is given the opportunity to use a knife and fork even if a spoon is easier. He will probably find child-sized cutlery easiest and to start with you can still let him use a spoon for difficult items such as peas. Practise using knives and forks as you play – perhaps by 'cooking' with play-dough and Plasticine. Or play a dice game with a fork, knife and a milky way. Take it in turns to throw the dice and when someone gets six, he eats as much of the bar as possible, cutting it with a knife and fork only. Meanwhile, the other players carry on trying to throw a six so that they can have a go at the cutting and eating. Let your child practise using a knife for spreading toast or sandwiches – this will be easier than cutting to start with. Stand behind your child as he sits at the dinner table and show him how to grip the cutlery. When he is ready to cut his own food up, start with easier items such as quiche or fish fingers before he tackles pizza or sausages.

Tricky task no. 8 – making decisions

You can give your child a lot of confidence and a feeling of independence if you involve her in some of the day-to-day decisions. For instance, let her decide what to wear, what to have for breakfast and what to play with. And do not criticise her decision, having allowed her to make it, even if she does end up wearing a striped orange skirt with her sister's pink spotty top. Let her join in with the family decisions too such as deciding where to go on holiday or what type of pet to buy. Listen to what your child is saying, show an interest and do not belittle her even if her suggestions are completely impractical! She will need to make some decisions at school, whether it is choosing an activity, a partner or a pudding. So make sure she is used to deciding things at home so that she does not end up dithering in the lunch queue or pondering over which partner to choose.

Tricky task no. 9 – asking for help

Your child will not be, or be expected to be, completely independent when he first starts school. Even if he can manage all the tricky tasks, he probably will not know where everything is and will need to ask for the toilet. Or he may need assistance because he has spilt his paint or fallen over in the playground. Your child should have the confidence to ask when he needs or does not know something. Encourage this at home by not anticipating his every need. Try not to provide your child with a drink before he asks or put the clothes he needs out ready. Make sure he needs to ask for things in the familiar environment of home to start with. Then encourage him to ask for things in shops (in your presence) or in the library. Being confident in speaking out while you are there will help your child ask the teacher when you are not there to back him up or prompt him.

Tricky task no. 10 – coping with specific needs

Your child may have to cope with something specific to him such as glasses, a hearing aid or an inhaler. Make sure the teacher is aware of this need and arrange who is to take control of any items such as medicine or an inhaler before he starts school. Wearing glasses is the most common specific need and your child is unlikely to be the only one in the class with them on. Make sure the teacher knows that he wears glasses (especially if he does not like wearing them) and whether he needs them all the time or just for close work. Give him a strong, named case to keep them in if they are not worn all the time. Your child will have his eyes tested at school, usually during the first year.

Traps to fall into – parents' questions

❝ *I think I've made my child too independent – he is quite happy to go off on his own now and talk to anyone.* ❞

You cannot make a child too independent but whatever his personality, he needs to be aware and protected from 'stranger danger' before he starts school. Even though you may be taking him in and collecting him each day, he will be outside to play, albeit supervised. And at home he may now be playing outside with friends. Set your own rules for what he is and is not allowed to do at home. This will largely depend on where you live but you may by now be allowing him to call on a friend in your street to play, provided

PREPARE YOUR CHILD FOR SCHOOL

he tells you first. Stick rigidly to whatever rules you make but explain *why* this is so important. Sadly, this will mean telling your child that not everyone in the world is kind and good. Include the rule, therefore, that if a stranger ever talks to your child, he must scream and run home or go straight back into the school. Tell him *never* to get into anyone's car without telling Mum or Dad first, even if it is someone he knows.

With increasing independence, your child will also need to know about road safety. Teach him to cross the road properly, letting him take the lead, with you at his side. Explain why he should never cross the road next to a parked car and insist he wears a helmet when he rides his bike, even if it is on the pavement.

> **(** *When we are in a hurry, I have to give my child a lot of help and then he expects me to do it for him the next time.* **)**

There is no doubt that doing it for him is usually a lot quicker and easier. When your child is learning to dress himself it can seem to take hours and when he washes his hands, filling the basin right to the top and using half a bar of soap, you wonder why he did not just have a bath while he was at it. During this time of learning new, independent skills, you will have to be patient, be prepared and start getting ready to go out a lot earlier. After all, the best way for your child to learn these skills is by trying and the best way you can help is by encouraging him, praising his efforts and giving him the minimal help needed; just enough to kerb his frustrations but not so much that you are doing it for him. Show your child how to tackle difficult tasks but do not take the easy option. However, you will need to be flexible – your child will obviously need more assistance when he is tired or unwell.

> **(** *What exactly will the teacher expect my child to be able to do for herself?* **)**

The teacher will expect your child to be able to enjoy playing with other children, showing some signs of co-operation, and to cope in school without you. She should be able to use the toilet independently and ask for it when she needs it. She should be able to (more or less) dress and undress herself, although some fastenings may still be difficult. She should be able to eat her lunch independently and occupy herself with an activity for more than ten minutes. If your child has any particular difficulty, you should discuss this with the teacher beforehand. Do not forget, though, that your child is still in the process of becoming more independent and there is still progress to be made during the first year at school.

> *My child just does not want to tidy up his room, even though he is now quite capable of doing it.*

One of the most important keys in helping your child on the road to independence is motivation. Your child has got to want to do things for himself rather than get you to help all the time. Some children have a naturally independent personality while others need more encouragement. The best way to encourage your child is to praise all his efforts and reward him when he achieves his goal. A smile and an enthusiastic 'Well done!' may be enough but if your child needs even more encouragement, you could try a star chart. With this, your child earns a star every time he tidies his room, or whatever your goal is. He should get a star for effort – do not expect too much straight away. Once he has achieved a certain number of stars, you could provide a treat such as a trip out or a special tea of jelly, ice-cream and cakes. Build up towards a goal in slow, careful stages. So, for example, with tidying his room, your child could start by just helping you. Then you could give him one specific task such as tidying his bed or putting his clothes neatly on the chair. Gradually build up towards the aim of your child tidying his room on his own, even if it is not quite up to your standards! However, do not be tempted to re-do some of his good work as you will only put him off. Praise all his efforts and if necessary do the bits he missed while he is at playgroup or outside with friends. Your child will certainly be expected to put things away tidily at school so it is never too soon to get him used to tidying-up.

PREPARE YOUR CHILD FOR SCHOOL

My child started acting like a baby when she started nursery – talking in a baby voice, sucking her thumb and even wetting herself once. Will the same thing happen when she starts school?

During the settling-in period at school, some children do show signs of regressive behaviour if they are not completely settled or feel insecure. There is no need to comment about it to your child although you might like to mention it to the teacher. Just take it as a sign that your child needs extra affection, reassurance and a chance to chat about anything that is worrying her. If your child had difficulty settling in at nursery, it does not necessarily follow that she will have difficulty settling in at school. After all, nursery is a preparation for school in itself. And if starting nursery was one of her first separations from you, then starting school may not be as difficult. If, however, your child finds any new situation hard to cope with, then you need to ensure that she is really well prepared for school, knows exactly what to expect when she gets there and perhaps gets that extra bit of reassurance from you.

Pay attention – helping your child to listen

When he first starts school, your child should be able to listen to a story of reasonable length and to pay attention to the teacher in order to do as she asks. However, listening skills and attention will still be developing and your child's teacher will know exactly how much to expect from an average four- or five-year-old and how to encourage the children who find listening particularly difficult. A child who is able to give his full attention when you talk to him, who can spend time looking at books and who listens to most of what you say is obviously ready and able to learn. A child who flits from toy to toy, crawls off your knee after only one page of a favourite story and never listens to you will firstly need help to build up his concentration. Of course, no child gives his undivided attention all the time and may have good concentration skills one day and pay no attention to anyone or anything the next. It is important to note how attention develops during the pre-school years and how to help your child if he seems to be a poor listener as school approaches.

How attention develops

Under threes

Your baby will start off by being very distractable – as soon as she hears a noise or sees another toy, her attention will switch to that. However, between the ages of one and two, children often go through a period of very rigid concentration. She will now concentrate so well on her toy that you will find it impossible to distract her. When she is interested in an activity, you may find that she does not listen to you at all and you will even wonder if she can hear you! You will need to get her attention first before you speak to her – she will not yet listen to you and carry on with her activity at the same time. Usually between the ages of about two and three years, your child's attention will become more flexible. She will be able to switch her attention from the activity to you and back to the activity again with a little help. You will still need to get her attention before speaking but she will stop and listen more readily. Although she will concentrate for long enough to enjoy a short story, the length of time she will listen for is still very limited.

Three to four years

By playgroup age, your child will be able to switch his attention more readily. He should be past the stage of flitting from toy to toy and should now become absorbed in longer stretches of meaningful play. He will concentrate for much longer, providing the activity interests him, so make sure that what you are saying is of interest and he should listen well. However, his attention span still has some limitations. Stories or television programmes that are too long or complicated will lose your child's attention quickly. There is also quite a variation between different children at this stage. Some have poorer concentration than others and still find it difficult to complete a task or listen to more than one short story at a time.

These children will clearly need more help and encouragement to improve their listening skills.

Four to six years

You will still find yourself shouting 'You're not even listening!' or 'Didn't you hear what I just said?', but over all, your child will be concentrating better and will be able to do two things at once – listening to you without taking the focus off what he is doing. He needs to be able to do this at school of course, as the teacher will be giving instructions such as 'Put your books away now' or 'Line up at the door, please' while your child is doing something else. She will also be giving him assistance with pencil and paper activities which will involve your child in listening and looking at his work at the same time. Your child should be concentrating for much longer now and completing tasks more readily.

Twenty listening games

Noise tapes

Record sounds around the house and out in the street or the voices of your family. Now play the sounds back to your child and see if she can identify them. Start with easy sounds such as the telephone ringing, the dog barking or the tap running. Then try more difficult ones such as starting the car, knocking on the door, eating crisps or the traffic going past.

Listening stories

Tell your child a story but give him something specific to listen out for. You could, for example, ask him to make the appropriate noise every time he hears the name of an animal.

Matching noise makers

Make pairs of noise makers so that you and your child end up with an identical set of four or five 'instruments'. You can try putting various substances into different containers – uncooked rice or macaroni, one marble, sugar, screwed up balls of paper or buttons, for instance. You then hide your noise makers behind a screen, shake one and see if your child can find a matching one from her set. Make the noises fairly different from each other to start with, then as your child gets good at the game, make them more and more similar so that closer listening is needed. Or you could try making a sequence of two or three sounds for her to copy.

Remember, remember

Give your child instructions to carry out while he plays with his toys. Play people or a farm set are ideal for this sort of activity. Start with short, simple instructions such as 'Put the cow and horse into the stable' or 'Put one man in the house and another one on the slide'. Then move on to even longer instructions such as 'Find the cow, the pig and the horse', 'Put the biggest pig inside the shed' or 'Put the man with the hat under his chair and find the baby'. But do not always be teacher, let your child give you some difficult commands too. He will love making them too hard for you!

Musical noises

This is a version of musical bumps but with some keen listening needed. Make some large pictures to represent sounds which are similar to each other. Try a big snake which says 'Ssss', a baby in a pram for 'Shhh', a dripping tap for 'T-t-t-t' and a rabbit with great big teeth who says 'Fffff'. Put the pictures out on the floor and turn on the music for your child and all her friends to dance to. When the music stops, shout out (or perhaps whisper) one of the sounds. The children then have to run and stand on the right picture.

Chinese whispers

A good game for a group of children, the family, or playing at a party. Everybody sits in a circle and you whisper a short sentence to the person on your right. She then whispers it to the next person and so it goes round until the last person says it out loud to see if it bears any resemblance to the original sentence. Take it in turns to think of the sentences and make them longer as you get good at the game.

Singing, listening and concentrating

Some songs require good listening skills and considerable concentration. Try, for example 'Head, shoulders, knees and toes' where you miss out a different part of the body for each verse. Or try something like 'Old Macdonald' where the sequence of animals to remember gets longer and longer.

You can only cross the river if . . .

This is another good game for listening in a group. Your child and her friends stand at one end of the room and you give instructions along the lines of 'You can only cross the river if you've got a white vest on' or 'You can only cross the river if you had sausages for dinner'. Then the children who qualify run across the room. Take it in turns to shout out the instructions.

Simon says . . .

This is the old game of asking your child (and his friends) to do something which they only do if you say 'Simon says' first. This needs a lot of concentration and is great fun.

Matching rhythms

You and your child have a drum (a couple of biscuit tins and wooden spoons are ideal). You tap out a rhythm and your child has to copy it. If she finds this too difficult, try instead to tap out the names of the family as you say them together, i.e. Em-ma, Jess-i-ca and so on.

Spot the mistake

Make sure your child is listening really carefully to a story by putting in deliberate mistakes. This works better with a story which your child knows well. So for instance, you could tell the story of 'The Three Bears' but say that they were eating cornflakes or that Daddy Bear said 'Who's been sleeping in my tree?'.

I went to market . . .

This is really a memory game but it is good for concentration and fun as well. Take it in turns to say 'I went to market and bought . . .' adding a new item to the list every time. If your child finds it difficult to think of things, cut out pictures from magazines and stick them on to individual cards. Then take a card every time it is your turn to add an item to the list.

Stop and listen

Does your child seem to be on the go all the time, perhaps talking non-stop? Get her to stop everything she is doing and really listen. What can she hear? Maybe the dog barking next door, traffic in the street or the fridge humming. Set her a challenge one night to remember the first thing she hears in the morning when she wakes up.

Story tapes

You can buy story tapes for your child to listen to, sometimes with an accompanying book. But why not make your own? Record yourself reading your child's favourite story onto a cassette. Bang a saucepan or ring a bell when it is time to turn over the page.

Fetching stories

Put a selection of toys and objects out on the table and then tell your child a story about a birthday or Christmas. Every time you mention a present, he has to run and fetch it. Make it more difficult by mentioning more than one present at a time.

Give me a clue

Hide objects, or a favourite snack, around the room for your child to find. Give him a clue to listen to such as 'It's behind the television' or 'It's next to something we sit on'. Make sure he is really listening by giving him some negative clues such as 'It's not under anything' or 'It's not near the fireplace'.

Blind man's buff

If your child does not mind having a scarf tied around his eyes so that he cannot see, then this game can be made into a good listening activity. Take it in turns to be blind so when your child has his turn, you make noises from wherever you are in the room. Your child has then to work out where the noise is coming from and come over to try and touch you. Make fairly quiet noises such as rustling a newspaper so that he has to stop and listen really hard.

Squeak, piggy, squeak

A good group or party game. Sit round in a circle and blindfold one child. She then has to grab hold of someone and say 'Squeak, piggy, squeak'. That person squeaks and the blindfolded child has to guess who she has found from the squeak she hears. She can get additional clues if necessary from feeling the chosen person with her hands.

Traffic lights

Get your children to walk or crawl about the room being cars. You are the traffic lights so that when you shout 'red', they must stop and sit down; on orange they just stop and on green they go, or carry on moving.

Loud and soft dancing

Put on some music for your child to dance to. When you turn the volume up, she must dance quickly with her hands up in the air and when you play the music quietly she must dance slowly with her hands down. You can make up other rules for this as you go along but the idea is to get your child to listen for and distinguish between loud and soft sounds.

Hyperactive or fidget-pot?

There is a very fine line between a very active, fidgety child and one who is truly hyperactive. Boys are six times more likely to be hyperactive than girls and about ten per cent of all boys show some degree of hyperactivity. However, only a small percentage of these are truly hyperactive in the sense that they will be difficult to manage at school, with their learning greatly affected. Many hyperactive children were difficult babies, crying more, getting irritable and frustrated and having disrupted sleep patterns. As toddlers they tend to be into everything, flitting from toy to toy and creating endless breakages. However, it must be remembered that many toddlers go through an active and distractable stage and only a few of these will go on to have problems at nursery or school. If your child has most of the following symptoms, then he is probably hyperactive.

- Does not listen. Forgets simple instructions.
- Impulsive and sometimes aggressive.
- Asks endless questions, usually repetitive as he does not always absorb or remember the answer.
- Over-active. Cannot settle at anything.
- Behaves badly, especially in crowds or a noisy environment.
- A messy eater. Clumsy and disorganised.
- Does not settle long enough at anything to learn from it.
- Accident-prone.
- Interrupts other people who are speaking. Forgets what he is saying.

How to help

- Cut out background noise whenever possible. Is anyone actually watching the television? Keep breakable objects out of reach.
- Get your child's attention by calling her name before you speak to her.
- Give your child a very structured routine each day to help her to know what to expect next and become more organised.
- Praise your child when she does settle at anything.
- Keep calm yourself even if you are really at the end of your tether – your child will respond to your agitation and tension.
- Ignore bad behaviour whenever possible but give your child extra attention when she is behaving well. You could even try a star chart to encourage good behaviour.

- Restrict junk food and additives in your child's diet. This is not always the cause of hyperactivity but a change of diet has helped some children.
- Do not expect too much too soon. Build up your child's attention span slowly, getting her to complete short simple tasks first.
- Have a break from your child occasionally – if your partner, a friend or relative can look after her now and then this will help you deal with your child more readily after a break. If you really cannot cope, ask your GP or health visitor to refer you for family therapy or perhaps to an educational psychologist.
- Explain your child's problems to the school before she starts there.

He just won't listen! – parents' questions

My child is easily distracted and never seems to finish what she has started.

Cut down extra noise in the background – perhaps yours is a house with a radio, record player or television always on. Then remove any other distractions – your child will probably find it easier to finish, say, a puzzle on a bare kitchen table than on a bedroom floor full of other toys. Give her tasks to start with which are quicker and easier – smaller pictures to colour in or a shorter story to listen to – and praise her when she does complete something. Now gradually build up the activities so that she has to concentrate for slightly longer. However, do not expect too much at this stage. Most pre-school children still need frequent changes of activity.

PAY ATTENTION - HELPING YOUR CHILD TO LISTEN

My child is sometimes a good listener but at other times, he fidgets, his mind wanders and he doesn't pay any attention at all.

Do not expect too much – even adults cannot listen and concentrate all the time. Children need to have plenty of opportunities just to run around the garden or day-dream. You may find that your child listens well to stories which are easiest for him to follow and concentrates well on the most straightforward activities, especially towards the end of the day. Do not forget that he will not be able to concentrate for as long on more difficult tasks and may just switch off altogether if the story or what you are saying is too complicated. So when his mind does wander, check that you are not expecting him to listen to something too difficult. You will also find that he will listen better to things which interest him and sometimes switch off out of boredom. The same goes for adults!

I have to call my child for tea over and over again and sometimes when I talk to him, I realise that he just isn't listening. Could he be deaf?

You would certainly want your health visitor or GP to check this out as there is always the chance that your child does have a fluctuating hearing loss, particularly if he gets a lot of coughs, colds or, in particular, ear infections. It could equally be that your child is going through a stage of rigid attention where he can only listen to and concentrate on one thing at a time. Alternatively, he may have 'selective deafness', hearing you perfectly well but deciding to ignore you altogether! You will remember that when the health visitor checked your child's hearing early on, she distracted him with a toy but removed that toy immediately, before making the noise behind. This is because the toy could be too distracting or interesting to make it worthwhile for him to look up at a much less interesting noise. Or your child could get so immersed in the toy that he would barely notice the noise at all. The same can happen when your child is watching television. It could either be more

PREPARE YOUR CHILD FOR SCHOOL

interesting than you or your child could be too immersed to notice you. While your child is going through this phase, you will need to get his attention before you speak to him. Make sure he looks at you first and maintain eye contact while you are talking.

> *I'm worried in case my child won't do as the teacher says.*

Children starting school will still be in the process of learning to listen and many of the activities will be to help them with this and to build up each child's attention span. The teacher will not, therefore, be surprised if your child does not always listen and will be helping her if listening is poor. Help build up your child's attention span with the games and activities described and make sure she gets some experience at a nursery or playgroup where she will get used to listening to an adult in a group situation. Some children are, in fact, rather different at school than at home. The teacher will be relatively new to your child and used to commanding an authority over a group of young children. This combination often means that children listen far more to their teacher than they have ever done to a parent at home!

> *My child is definitely very active after eating certain foods. Is there a special diet I should try?*

There is no absolute proof that food allergies can cause hyperactivity or changes in behaviour but many people believe that a change of diet has helped their child. You could try cutting out foods with a lot of additives or colouring, or else you could cut out each food one at a time until you notice a difference. Give your child at least two weeks of additive-free food or a diet without a particular item before you decide whether cutting it out has helped. You could also contact the Hyperactive Children's Support Group (the address is at the back of the book), which will give you further information about specific diets. Your GP may refer you to a dietician, normally based at a hospital, who can advise you further.

CHAPTER SEVEN

Toys and equipment – what to buy and make

Right from the start, you will be buying toys and books for your child, hoping you have chosen something she will both enjoy and learn from. There are few parents who have not made at least one mistake, buying an exciting-looking toy which was then played with for 20 minutes only to spend the next five years in the cupboard. Most of us have watched our children on Christmas morning getting more fun out of the packaging than the toy that was once inside. And it is a rare child who does not seem to prefer the toys at playgroup or in the house next door to her own. Mind you, when you dash out and buy those favourite toys, her interests suddenly change and you collect yet more toys for the back of the cupboard. So before you buy anything else, consider the following.

Golden rules of toy buying

Never impulse buy

Always consider *why* are you buying a toy for your child. It may be for a birthday or Christmas in which case you have a chance to give the choice some considered thought as the event approaches. In between these special occasions, you may feel your child needs something else – perhaps he is bored with or has grown out of his present toys. In this case, choose what is clearly missing from his collection whether it is a physically demanding toy for outside or a turn-taking game for indoors.

Never buy out of guilt – working mums are very susceptible to this – or because your child is screaming or shouting for something in a shop. Beware of passing fads, either your child's or something you are bombarded with by television.

Listen to your child

Each child has its preferences and there is no point buying, say, puzzles for a child who hates them just because you think they will be good for her. Instead, think of other toys and games to help her with manipulation and visual skills. Your child will be the worst impulse buyer, pointing to something colourful and eye-catching in the shop accompanied by a loud 'I want' or 'I've *always* wanted one of those!'. It is far better to observe your child at playgroup or playing at a friend's and see what really interests her. Some shops have sample toys put out for your child to try and this may give you a clearer indication of what her current needs and interests are.

Choose fun toys

It is so easy to get caught up with the intellectual and educational content of a toy that the fun value is forgotten. Toys are for your child to enjoy and although he will, and should, learn from them, this will happen effortlessly while he is having fun.

Choose toys to last

Not only do toys need to be tough and long-lasting physically, they also need to be suitable for your child now and in at least six months' time, preferably longer. A shape-sorter or puzzle which your child can do easily may bore your child in a matter of weeks. However, some toys have much longer-lasting play value because your child can do more with them as she develops. Bricks are a good example of this. A two-year-old will enjoy building towers with you and knocking them down, a three-year-old might sort them into colours, sizes or shapes, a four-year-old will do some more adventurous building while a five-year-old may combine them with her animals or play people to build a farm or hospital.

Choose toys with educational value

These are more than the obvious ones which deal with pre-reading or writing skills. If a toy addresses physical development or imagination, it is educational as well. Just ensure that the range of toys your child has covers the following areas of development:

Physical	Both toys of large movements (bikes, balls) and of small manipulative movements (puzzles, scissors).
Imaginative	Any pretend toys from pots and pans to toy telephones.
Intellectual	Toys which require real thought – matching games, magnetic letters and, of course, books.
Creative	Paint, play-dough, musical instruments.
Experimental	Sand and water toys.

Of course, some toys come into more than one category which usually means their play and learning value is very good.

Ask yourself if something else would be better

In some cases, not only would something home-made do, it would be better. This particularly applies to toys for imaginative play. Your child can do far more with a cardboard box than a pretend cooker, for example. Not only does your child need to use more imagination with the box, but when he has finished cooking, the box can be a car, bus, shop counter or anything else he can think of. Similarly, children use more imagination with socks as puppets, with your old clothes to dress up in rather than bought outfits, and with shoe boxes made into dolls' houses. You can buy any activity ready made these days but how much more fun rummaging through the kitchen drawers for collage materials than buying a box of them. And how much more thought is needed to make a shop out of empty packets than out of a ready-made set.

Choose toys to share

Some toys lend themselves to group play better than others. Ensure that your child has some toys which can be played with another child or even *have* to be played with someone else. Obvious choices are bat and ball games and board games. Of course, your child will need time on her own too so something like Duplo bricks or play people is ideal as these can be played with together or alone. On the other hand, swings, bikes, drawing boards and puzzles are largely for solitary play although they can help your child with turn taking.

Do choose some toys with emotional value

Most pre-school children need some comforter, which may be a blanket, thumb or special toy. The toy is likely to be a teddy or soft toy and carting it around everywhere may not have much play value but clearly fulfils a need in your child. Soft toys can, in fact, be used for imaginative play and many pre-school children make them talk as well as eat and sleep. Both girls and boys enjoy pretend play with dolls and teddies and the wheelbarrow will become a pram or the shoe box a bed.

Choose toys at the right level

Choose toys that are too easy for your child and they will not last very long, but choose activities which are too difficult and frustration sets in. A good toy or game should be flexible enough for children of differing ages to enjoy. For example, cards with letters printed on are boring for children who know their letters and of no interest to children who are not ready to learn them. However, if you buy magnetic letters, even a very young child can enjoy sticking them on the fridge or fishing them up with magnetic fishing rods. She can then go on to learn the names of letters and much later still, spell out her name on the fridge door. Similarly, difficult constructional toys will frustrate a young child but a simpler one like Duplo can be managed at an early age and then added to as your child grows and develops.

Choose safe toys

Make sure the toy has a symbol on it to indicate that it has passed the EC Standard (EN71) or the British Standard (BS 5665). One of these numbers, the symbol 'CE' or a lion symbol indicates that the toy is safe. In addition to this, toys with small parts which could be swallowed should say 'Not suitable for children under three years'. If your four-year-old still puts toys into his mouth, you may want to supervise play with these items. Always supervise your child when he is playing with water or balloons. Check toys regularly for damage and be particularly careful if you buy home-made or second-hand toys.

Toy essentials

Each child has his own preferences and every family has its own budget, but the following items should feature in every collection of toys.

Books	Home-made, bought and library books.
Play-dough or Plasticine	Make your own by mixing two cups of flour, a teaspoonful of salt, a cup of water, food colouring and two tablespoons of oil in a large pan. Stir over a gentle heat.

PREPARE YOUR CHILD FOR SCHOOL

Sand	You do not need a large sand pit. A lined covered hole in the garden or even a bucket will do.
Sand and water toys	Old (safe) cooking utensils and empty plastic bottles are fine. Use them in the bath too.
Scissors and glue	And old magazines, catalogues and material to cut and stick. Choose safe, round-ended scissors.
Music	Home-made instruments, cassette tapes or just the family for a sing-song.
Dice	Dice can be home-made (out of a box) with the usual dots or else written numbers.
Building bricks	And later more complex constructional toys such as Lego.
Science toys	A magnet, a packet of seeds, a mirror and a magnifying glass lead to hours of discovery and fun.
Pretend toys	Dolls and teddies to start with, then miniature people – Lego, play people or Duplo people are ideal.
Magnetic numbers and letters	Make a fishing rod with a magnet at the end to make a game of learning letters.

Pencils and crayons	Plus paint, felt pens and plenty of scrap paper.
Cars	For girls and boys. Preferably with people who fit inside and a road mat (bought or home-made).
Board game	For taking turns. A matching lotto game can be made out of two identical catalogues.
Puzzles	Or cut up pictures to re-assemble.
Threading games	Uncooked macaroni and string is fine.

Never throw away

boxes big enough to sit in
shoe boxes
egg boxes
empty toilet rolls
any other empty cartons
old (safe) kitchen utensils
your old clothes, especially hats
old socks
newspaper
paper with a blank side
card (including empty cereal boxes)

PREPARE YOUR CHILD FOR SCHOOL

Which book?

There are more children's books available than ever before and whether you are borrowing one out of the library or buying one, make sure that you make the right choice. Above all, books should be exciting for your child, whatever her age. If she learns to love books, she will soon want to read. So how do you choose out of the hundreds of books available?

- Choose one at the right level, not a difficult one your child might grow into. You will not want to put her off books. For under threes, choose an easy-to-follow book with plenty of pictures which does not last longer than she can concentrate. Then build up from there.

- Follow your child's interests. If he loves dinosaurs, choose a story about a dinosaur. If he watches a particular series on television, get the accompanying book.

- Bright colourful pictures are important as they encourage your child to look at the story by himself, even before he can read.

- Choose varied books. Some stories, some factual books, some songs and poems and some alphabet and counting books.

- If the language is too complicated for your child, simplify it until he knows the story well. Then explain any difficult or new words.

- At first choose stories that can be read as a whole in one go. Once your child is about five, she will begin to enjoy stories told in more than one episode.

- Take as many books out of the library as you are allowed. Choose one or two you are sure about and experiment with the rest. However, do not force your child to listen to them — if they prove unsuitable, put them to one side and read the others as many times as she likes.

- Let your child have the fun of choosing her own library book. Most children quite naturally choose something appropriate.

- When your child is at the stage of recognising words, choose books with repetitive lines in. You could even choose a story with her name in.

- Do not feel you always have to be buying new books. Children love the same stories over and over again and are more likely to tell stories themselves by looking at the most familiar books.
- Any book – or comic – which your child enjoys is a good one, as it is enthusiasm for books which leads to enthusiasm for reading. Beware of imposing your own choices of books on your child. Do show her books which you feel she might enjoy but let the final choice be hers.

Before you shop – parents' questions

❝ *Is there anything I should* not *buy for my four-year-old son?* ❞

Firstly, beware of toys which have little or no versatility. You can only do one thing with something like a rocking horse so the play value is limited. Also, think carefully about buying guns and swords – they may lead to aggressive play and as children of this age do not always make a clear distinction between fact and fantasy, violence and aggression may seem like a game. It is sometimes tempting to rush out and buy something you have seen at your child's playgroup, particularly if it is his favourite toy there. If he is spending three mornings a week at the group, then it may be better to widen his experience and buy him something different for home. Do not be tempted to buy books or games which he does not really want but which *you* think would be good for him. The sex of your child should not be a restriction on what you buy for him. Unfortunately, it is often the case that girls have fewer constructional toys and boys have fewer 'pretend' toys like cookers. So make sure that your child has access to both to develop all his or her skills. You will know whether buying anything breakable is suitable for your own child or not!

Is watching television or videos educational for my pre-school child?

It can be, but watching television for long periods is very passive and after a while your child may lose concentration but still remain sitting in front of it, not taking anything in at all. Check that your child really is listening and understanding by asking her about the programme she has just watched. Ideally, a parent should watch with the child so that they can discuss what is happening. Teach your child to be selective right from the start. Look in the paper together and read out what is going to be on. Choose one or two suitable programmes and just watch those. Do not be tempted to leave it switched on just because your child seems occupied. Children can learn a lot from pre-school programmes and if you have a video, this is ideal as, like books, children enjoy the same programmes over and over again.

Does my four-year-old need a computer?

Your child will almost certainly have some access to a computer when he starts school. Having a computer before then is unlikely to push your child ahead of the others but if you were thinking of getting a computer anyway, the sooner the better. However, you may prefer to wait until you can invest in a computer which will last your child for many years, taking him up to when he might do word processing or even write his own programs. In the early years, having a computer in the home can give you and your child confidence. He will soon become familiar with loading in the program, the keyboard and some of the vocabulary associated with computers such as 'program', 'mouse' or 'loading'. Make sure the pre-school software is fun with interesting graphics, as well as educational.

Some computer games are suitable for more than one child, which can make them more social pieces of equipment. For, like the television, there is a danger of your child sitting in front of the computer for hours while both social and imaginative play take a back seat. Beware of computerised electronic learning aids which may be cheaper than a computer but are not as versatile. Your child may learn the limited activities quickly and so grow out of the aid sooner than a computer.

> *Should I buy the books from the reading scheme my child will be doing at school?*

No. She will start on the reading scheme as soon as the teacher feels she is ready and then a reading book will almost certainly be sent home. There is no advantage to buying anything which your child will be doing at school; you would be better concentrating on the pre-three Rs activities outlined in chapter 10. If your child is ready to read, you may want to build up a small sight vocabulary and make your own books using these words. Doing very obvious school work at home may make your child feel she is being pressurised to succeed. Always go at your child's own pace and go on to the next step when she is ready. Once your child has settled in at school, you can then ask the teacher if there is anything you can buy to help her at home, especially if she has any particular difficulty in a specific area.

> *What is a toy library?*

You can contact the Toy Libraries Association (the address is at the back of the book) to find out if there is one in your area. Some are only made available to children with special needs but others are available to everyone. They work in exactly the same way as a book library although a donation is sometimes appreciated when you borrow a toy.

CHAPTER EIGHT

Making friends – good social skills and behaviour

When your child starts school, she should already have had plenty of opportunity to mix with other children of the same age. Although the friends she will make as a pre-school child may not be as lasting or as strong as those formed at school, they are essential if she is to learn to be a co-operative and social child. By school age, your child should have begun to see things from another's point of view – understanding how the other child would feel if she hit out at him, for example. She should be playing co-operatively and be able to share and take turns. She should also be showing signs of empathy, giving affection to a child who has fallen off his bike, for instance. Of course, there will still be episodes of snatching, shouting and total unco-operation but over all your child will enjoy the company of others and look forward to making new friends at school.

Your child should also have developed some of the social niceties, from saying 'Please' and 'Thank you' to using a hanky instead of a sleeve. And she should be able to form appropriate relationships with adults as well as children. Obviously, if your child has any particular behaviour problem, whether tantrums, being aggressive or even swearing, this will affect the way she socialises and makes friends at school. Before school, therefore, help your child curb any anti-social behaviour, encourage her to form good relationships with other children and adults and above all help her have fun with children at home and in a pre-school group.

The best of friends: how friendships are made

Under threes

Children of this age undoubtedly enjoy the company of others of the same age, but co-operative play is rare. In fact, they tend to play alongside rather than with each other. They also have little idea of sharing or turn-taking and consequently there tends to be a lot of snatching going on. Adult intervention is therefore necessary, with a brief and simple explanation of *why* we do not hit, snatch and so on. As children's communication abilities are still limited, you may find that they push another child out of the way or grab rather than ask for something. Asking instead of forcing will need encouragement from this early age, so start showing your child how to say 'Excuse me' or 'Can I have a go now?' even if you do not get much success to start with.

Three to four years

During this time, children start to play in a much more co-operative way. They now have the communication skills to discuss their play and make decisions about it – so you will hear 'You be Mummy and I'll be the baby' or 'This box can be a car, OK?'. Children start to form real friendships, showing a preference for particular children and seeking them out at playgroup or nursery. Of course, some children will be more social than others at this age, depending both on development and personality. Some will enjoy being in a bigger group of children but many will particularly enjoy one-to-one relationships either at home or within that group. Children may begin to share and take turns now but will seem self-centred and selfish a lot of the time. They will need a lot of praise when they do share and co-operate, and will respond to explanations of *why* we share.

Four to six years

By the time children start school, they should show sure signs of considering others – though they will not be considerate all the time! As well as sharing and taking turns in organised games, children are now able to see things from the point of view of another child. They can understand how another child feels if he is hurt, left out or bullied. However, they will still need guidance in using this co-operation and will be expected to carry out activities in pairs or small groups in the classroom in order to develop good social and communication skills.

How to help

- Give your child the chance to develop friendships. Make sure she has the opportunity to attend a pre-school group and encourage her to invite friends home to play. Make a point of visiting friends with children so that your child has the chance to play with one other child or in a small group as well as in the larger group her nursery or playgroup provides.
- Let your child choose her own friends. Even three-year-olds will show a marked preference for particular children. Take your child's lead in this, rather than forcing a friendship because *you* like the other child or are particularly friendly with the parents.
- If your child is shy and does not mix well with other children, she may be better playing with one child at a time to start

with. Invite a child round, but play with them too at first, backing off once they feel more settled with each other.

- Buy your child a pet or plant to help her consider other living things – ideally this will expand so that she will be caring towards other children. A pet does not have to be a cat or a dog, even looking after a goldfish or stick insect will help show that caring for others is rewarding.

- Assert yourself if a new neighbour moves in with children of similar ages to your own. Go and knock on the door as soon as you can to introduce yourself and the children.

- If you have more than one child, encourage the friendship between them. Make a point of praising them whenever they help each other or play games together in a friendly and co-operative way.

- Avoid comparing your child with her friends, especially in front of her as it may affect self confidence. If you want children to be good friends, then they should not feel too competitive with each other.

- Do not expect too much from very young children as sharing and playing together are skills which need to be learned – they do not always come automatically.

- As your child gets older and more verbal, do not always interfere when she argues with a friend – give them a chance to sort it out between themselves first.

- Do not feel your child *always* needs to be playing with friends or brothers and sisters. Allow her some time and space to play quietly on her own each day.

Taking turns

When your child starts school, he will need to be able to take turns in an organised game and know how to lose without tears or tantrums. You can start helping him with this skill from an early age.

- Play turn-taking games with your child which do not involve winning or losing. Perhaps you could each take a turn at going down the slide or rolling a hula-hoop along. Make a point of saying 'I've had my turn, now it's your turn' and so on.
- Once your child can take turns with you, help her to take turns with another child but under your supervision to start with. If your child has a friend round and they both want to play on the trike, for instance, explain how one child can go up and down the drive as one turn and then the other child can have her turn. Talk about fairness and sharing as you explain.
- Now see if your child can take turns with friends but with minimal intervention from you. If arguing starts, act as referee but see if they can decide between themselves how they are going to take turns.
- Play simple board games with your child; anything from picture lotto to snakes and ladders. Talk about whose turn it is as you go along. Never make a big thing about who wins and loses and do not always let your child win on purpose. If he is very competitive and a bad loser, explain that you enjoyed the game and it does not matter who wins. Set an example by being a good loser yourself and praise your child when he does lose gracefully.
- Once your child can play board games fairly with you, encourage him to play them with friends, although you may need to supervise at first.

Sharing

Start teaching your child to share from an early age, but do not expect too much if she is under three. Once she is at school, not only will she have to share the equipment and the teacher but she will certainly be regarded as a friendly and social child if she can share her snack at play time.

- Set an example. Do not be seen to squabble with your partner over which television programme to watch; and if someone gives you a box of chocolates, share them round.
- The first person your child will be able to share with is you. When she has some sweets or crisps, for example, encourage her to give you one and make a point of giving her a big thank you and a hug by way of praise. Extend this so that she shares things round the whole family and make sure the other members of the family share in this way too.
- Sharing treats should become automatic and so should sharing toys when friends come to play. However, do not expect too much too soon. Very precious toys may be too difficult to share to start with so it might be worth putting them out of sight to avoid arguments. When a friend comes, explain to your child that they will *both* be playing with her toys just as she would expect to play with her friend's toys at his house.
- Buy two children a bag of sweets or crisps to share between them rather than one bag each.
- Praise your child every time she shares with another child and explain the reasons why we share.

Co-operative play

Working and playing together is an important part of school life and your child will be learning a lot about co-operation when she takes part in classroom activities and plays team games. There are some useful games and activities you can do at home to set her on the road to good co-operative play.

- Choose toys which require children to play together in a co-operative way. Guns and weapons may just lead to aggressive play and two dolls may just mean playing alongside each other. Play people, a farm set or building bricks are more likely to help children play and talk together.

- As your child gets older, choose toys and games which most definitely require more than one player. Bat and ball games or board games may be suitable.

- A good game for a group of children is to set them a challenge with a sheet of paper or a mat. Simply put the paper on the floor and then tell the children that they all have to get one foot and one hand on the paper. The smaller the paper and the bigger the group of children, the more difficult the challenge and the more verbal co-operation needed. The children will soon learn that to meet the challenge, they will need to work together and discuss how they are going to organise themselves.

- Set another challenge with a bottle or narrow-topped container and some corks on the end of string. The corks (or crayons) need to be slightly narrower than the neck of the bottle but not so narrow that two can be pulled out together. Put the corks or crayons in the bottle with the strings hanging out – one for each child. Explain that when you say 'Go!', they have to get the corks out of the bottle. Obviously if they all pull together, nobody will succeed. This will therefore involve co-operation, taking turns and joint discussion.

- Encourage games which require a lot of talking. 'Shops' is ideal or maybe older children could act out a familiar story such as 'The Three Bears' or 'The Three Little Pigs'. If your child snatches or is aggressive, explain how asking works better. Encourage her to say, by demonstrating, 'Please can I play with that next? rather than grabbing or 'Who wants to be the wolf?' or, 'Shall we take turns being the wolf?' rather than 'I'm the wolf, so there!'.

Being bad

It is extremely unlikely that your child will always behave impeccably. It may even be that, at times, he is downright naughty. Many parents worry about bad behaviour as school approaches in case it affects both his progress and the teacher's attitude towards their child. Children in the first year of primary school are not going to behave perfectly all the time and teachers are used to dealing with inappropriate behaviour, sometimes in consultation with home. However, when your child starts school, he should at least know how to behave and what is and is not acceptable. Hopefully, he will have developed some sense of right and wrong by then and feel guilty and sorry if he does get carried away and behave badly.

As your child grows up, attitudes towards his behaviour will vary. Some people consider naughtiness in a three-year-old just part of growing up, some even find it positively endearing. At the same time, others will describe a toddler who frequently disobeys as anything from 'naughty' to 'defiant' and 'difficult'. It must be remembered that an action, such as hitting another child, may have been done out of a different motive to the obvious one. A baby of eight or nine months may simply be greeting another child, a two-year-old may want a toy that another child has and has no other way of asking for it, and a five-year-old may hit another child because he does not like him and wants to hurt him. Only the five-year-old is really being bad – the younger children are still in the process of learning that hitting is wrong. They will get that sense of right and wrong from their parents and it is never too soon to start with a consistent and age-appropriate method for dealing with being bad.

Being good

How you teach your child to be good will largely depend on her age and why she has done something naughty. A young baby who is fiddling with a socket is not being naughty if she has no concept of its danger. However, you will want to show her immediately that she must not do this with a firm 'No!'. If your child is being naughty to attract attention, then you may want to ignore it but give more attention next time she is being good. Or if your child is testing you out to see how far she can go, then you will want to ensure that your responses are firm and consistent. Of course, some children may be naughty out of unhappiness or stress, sometimes following a major change in their life. This could be starting school, but whatever the reason, you will probably want to treat the cause rather than the behaviour, discussing the problem with your child and tackling it together. The following methods of encouraging good behaviour may be appropriate to your child, although her age and personality need to be taken into account when deciding which regime to adopt. In fact, you will probably use a combination of these methods at any one time.

Set an example

You will have noticed how your child loves to vacuum 'just like Mummy' (or Daddy) and wants to wear make-up and aftershave. The same thought and logic can be applied to other types of behaviour but it is not so cute if she wants to swear, argue, smoke or lose her temper 'just like Mummy'. Setting an example means letting your child see you being kind and considerate. It means not letting her see you lying to a neighbour that you cannot help because you are going on a non-existent outing. It means not letting your child see you being aggressive – even towards her. For if you hit your child, you are setting an example whether you want to or not. You also need to be aware that other people will be setting examples and these may include favourite television characters, who consistently demonstrate that aggression is somehow fun.

Explaining the reason

Young children tend to judge how naughty something is by how cross a parent is. If you ask a toddler why hitting another child is naughty, he will invariably say 'Because Mummy will get cross'. But by school age, you will want your child to know exactly why something is wrong so that he develops a conscience. Right from the start, give simple explanations such as 'Don't hit Barry, you'll hurt him' or 'Don't tear your book or you won't have it to read tomorrow'. 'Because I say so' is not a reasonable explanation. Some reasons will need to be given after a child has calmed down and stories can be used to discuss naughtiness in general. So you can ask your older child, 'How do you think Cinderella felt?' or 'Should Goldilocks have eaten the Bears' porridge?'.

Rewarding good behaviour, ignoring the bad

Your child needs feedback from you when she is being good just as much, if not more, than when she is being naughty. It is so easy to reprimand naughty behaviour but to just ignore your child when she is playing nicely on her own. This pattern will obviously mean that your child gets more attention for being naughty than for being good. So instead reward good behaviour and ignore the bad. When your child is playing nicely, tell her how pleased you are and give her extra affection and some of your time. When she is walking round the supermarket sensibly then praise her and perhaps buy her a favourite snack, explaining why she deserves it. But if she misbehaves at the supermarket, screaming for sweets or knocking things off the shelf, then strap her into the seat and give her no attention whatsoever until she is quiet – then chat together as if nothing had happened.

Removing your child to a solitary area

This is useful for temper tantrums when your child needs a chance to cool down. It can also give you a chance to cool down, particularly if you are tempted to hit your child but do not want to. This is very immediate, does not give your child undue attention and can be very effective. So if, for example, your child is pushing another child outside, bring him in and sit him on a chair facing the wall for ten minutes (this seems a long time to a pre-school child). Then he can return to play, but be consistent and sit him on the 'naughty chair' every time he pushes. Some parents send their child to their bedroom, which is based on the same principle.

Be careful, though, that he does not come to associate his bedroom with a place of punishment and therefore unpleasant feelings.

Removing the cause

If your child is tearing a book, you will obviously take it away. If she is flicking paint on the wall, she will not be allowed to finish her painting and if she is being aggressive to another child at his house, she can be taken home. This is immediate and effective for situations which cannot be ignored.

Denying future treats

This is where you say 'We are not going to the park/having ice-cream because you have been naughty'. This is not suitable for a very young child who may not see the connection between her behaviour and your punishment. Otherwise it is an effective non-aggressive punishment. You can, of course, give it as a threat to start with to give your child one more chance, but once you say a treat is to be withdrawn, stick to it if you want credibility next time.

To hit or not to hit

Hitting is immediate and usually stops bad behaviour straight away. It is often not so effective in the long term and you are just as likely to get bad behaviour the next time. It is also teaching your child to solve problems with aggression and is giving his behaviour a lot of attention. Children who receive physical reprimands may develop lying as a way of trying to avoid punishment. If you do use physical punishment on your child, he will become more aggressive himself.

A taste of her own medicine

This is where you pull your child's hair to show her how it feels. This, again, leads to a more aggressive child. Your child *knows* how it feels so use verbal explanations instead. Say something like

MAKING FRIENDS – GOOD SOCIAL SKILLS AND BEHAVIOUR

'Look, Sophie's crying because you hurt her. You know how it hurts to have your hair pulled, don't you?'.

Withdrawal, or threat of withdrawal, of love

To tell your child that you do not like him because he has been naughty is not very effective and he is likely to become anxious and withdrawn with very low self-esteem. Just concentrate on showing him how much you love him when he is being good.

Being consistent

You will find the best way of dealing with your child's behaviour but whatever the method, she should expect the same response every time she does something wrong. So do not tell your child off for something one day but let her do it the next, although you may want to be flexible at times of stress, illness or tiredness. Liaise with your partner and anyone else involved in her upbringing so that, as far as possible, you are all consistent with each other.

Anti-social? – parents' questions

❝ *My child is always telling fibs. His teacher will not know what to believe.* ❞

Three- and four-year-olds nearly always go through a phase of telling lies and these usually involve denying something that they have done to avoid getting into trouble. They sometimes also tell exaggerated stories to impress friends or gain attention. This can involve anything from saying they have got a pet giraffe to describing Daddy as 'taller than a house'. These may just be inventive fantasies and nothing to worry about but if you feel the lying is compulsive and an indication of insecurity, you should tackle the problem. As for denial of bad deeds, you will need to explain to your child why lying is wrong. For older children, you can include an explanation of how people stop trusting and believing those who frequently lie. Discuss a lie or exaggeration with your child when it occurs. Give him a chance to explain why he lied, if he can, and then forget about it. Avoid interrogating or cross-examining your child as it may make him more determined to stick to his lie. Give him the opportunity to confess rather than attempt to wring the truth out of him. If your child does own up, do praise him, particularly if it comes unprompted. Always keep your reactions appropriate. If your child breaks your best vase quite accidentally, this should make you less angry than if he were to throw an old unwanted plate on the floor on purpose. Accept that some accidents and breakages will occur although some reprimand may be needed. However, you do not want your child to lie out of fear of your reaction. If you feel that your child's exaggerated lies are getting out of hand, ignore them but boost your child's self-esteem by praising his achievements.

> ❝ My child's manners are often appalling. I have to remind her to say "please" and "thank you" every time. ❞

Make sure you are setting an example so that your child always hears *you* saying 'please', 'thank you' and 'excuse me'. Explain to your child why we should be polite so she understands that she should treat other people how she would like to be treated; and that people like and accept polite children. Praise or even reward your child when she is polite and ignore bad manners if she seems to be doing it to get your attention. Insist on 'please' and 'thank you' to the point of ignoring her requests when she omits 'please' and removing her drink if she does not say 'thank you' when she gets it. It is important for you and your partner to agree on the manners you expect from your child. It is no good one of you saying that elbows must be kept off the table, if the other does not mind.

> ❝ My child has some disgusting habits, including picking his nose! ❞

MAKING FRIENDS – GOOD SOCIAL SKILLS AND BEHAVIOUR

He certainly will not be the only one starting school with this habit but it is worth tackling it now. Sit down and explain to your child why it is disgusting – you could even point out another child doing it (out of earshot) to get your child to agree with you. Make sure your child always has a hanky on him and if necessary show him how to keep his nose well blown (see page 63). Remind him to use his hanky every time you see a finger heading towards a nostril but do not worry – his class-mates will set him right if you fail!

> *My child has an imaginary friend. I've even found myself setting the table for her. What is the teacher going to make of it when she starts school?*

Most children drop their imaginary friends once they have started school and even if they do not, the friend does not usually go to school with them. In fact, if you ask the teacher at nursery or play group about your child's imaginary friend, you may find that she is not even aware that your child has one. This suggests that your child has a pretend friend as a substitute for the real thing: it is certainly more common amongst only children. Make sure, then, that your child has plenty of opportunity to mix with other children. However, it should not be thought of as a problem as such, so carry on laying the table and do not reprimand your child for it. Recent research suggests that children with imaginary friends in early childhood go on to be creative and intelligent adults.

> *My child has become very aggressive recently and is something of a bully at his nursery.*

Explain to your child why being aggressive is unacceptable. Try to get him to see things from the other child's point of view by talking about what it feels like to be pushed or hit. Discuss how to ask for things and sort problems out verbally. Your child may have difficulty knowing exactly how to relate to other children. Try inviting one child back to your house to play – your child may find it easier to curb his aggression in a one-to-one situation than in a group. If your child is aggressive, remove him from the situation by sitting him in the equivalent of 'the corner' or sending him upstairs. Never hit your child for being aggressive – this makes no sense at all; and make sure he is not copying aggression from anyone in the family. Encourage him to play with constructive toys rather than destructive ones. Playing with guns and swords or watching violence on television will in all probability lead to more aggressive behaviour from your child. Some aggressive children have very low self-esteem. Boost his confidence by praising achievements and give him extra attention when he is being kind to others or affectionate to you.

CHAPTER NINE

Which pre-school group?

An increasing number of children attend some form of pre-school group, whether it is a nursery or playgroup, and the majority of parents and teachers consider this essential as part of preparing for school. A pre-school group should offer an enjoyable, safe and structured environment for children to meet others of the same age, and to learn and develop through play, gradually becoming more independent and ready for school. Half of all three- and four-year-olds in Britain attend playgroups, most of which are set up and partly run by parents. Other children attend state-run or private nurseries or day nurseries. The majority of children attend for one or two years before starting school although children going to a private nursery, particularly when both parents are working, may start a lot sooner. The main aims of most pre-school groups are to prepare your child for school and give him the opportunity to socialise with other children. How these aims are tackled will vary from nursery to nursery and from playgroup to playgroup. Every group will have its own policies and aims and it is essential that you choose one to suit your child as well as your circumstances.

State-run nursery schools and classes

These usually take children for the year before starting school, although some may take children from three years. A nursery class is part of an infant or primary school but is otherwise the same as a nursery school. The classes within a primary school may take children from a catchment area wider than the school so that some of the children will eventually move on to other schools. The availability of state-run nursery places depends entirely on where you live and there are few places in the country where a nursery place is guaranteed for all pre-school children. Some areas work on a first come, first served basis but most will take the eldest children first so whether you get a place depends on your child's date of birth. Children with particular educational, medical or social needs may also be offered a priority place. Most children attend on a part-time basis, usually three to five mornings or afternoons a week, with sessions lasting two-and-a-half or three hours.

Nursery schools are generally more formal than playgroups although the emphasis is still very much on learning through play. They are run by trained nursery teachers, usually in conjunction with an assistant who may be a nursery nurse. The children do some activities as a whole group such as listening to a story, singing and snack time and the sessions will have a definite structure. However, the children probably will not be doing any formal learning of letters, numbers or writing although some of these skills may come up during other games and activities. Children will certainly be preparing for school, socialising with others and learning to be part of a group.

Private nursery schools

These vary enormously in size, length of sessions, fees and curriculum so you need to visit each one to find out more. Many take children from as young as two or two-and-a-half and the sessions may sometimes be longer (three to three-and-a-half hours) than in state-run nurseries. There may also be more flexibility than state nursery schools in the number of sessions you take and they may therefore be more suited to families where both parents work. Some have a less formal curriculum with the emphasis on learning through play while others teach reading, writing and maths skills, allowing more able children to attempt tasks normally started in the first year of primary school. Some even do gym, French or recorder classes. Private nursery schools are usually run by trained nursery teachers with assistants. Some aim to prepare your child for a private school and even have a uniform. Places are usually offered on a first come, first served basis although in some cases, parents and children are interviewed first.

Montessori nurseries

Some private nurseries are run according to the Montessori philosophy. The Montessori method is a child-centred approach, with each child being allowed to develop at his own pace. There is specific equipment associated with the philosophy which helps each child to learn through experience and play. There is a particular emphasis on practical life activities and courtesy. The atmosphere is calm and the sessions organised in a highly structured way.

State-run day nurseries

These cater for working parents and are often open from 7.30 am until about 6.00 pm all the year round with children attending from as young as three months. Priority places are given to families with particular social or medical problems. Otherwise it is difficult to get a place. They are run by Social Services and are staffed by nursery nurses, not teachers.

Private day-nurseries

These offer the same facilities as state day nurseries and cater for families where both parents work. In areas where there is little or no state provision, you will need to book your place early. They are usually run by nursery nurses and have to be registered with Social Services and meet an appropriate standard.

Playgroups

These often have similar curricula to nursery schools but may be less formal and without a set structure to the session. Most are affiliated to the Pre-School Playgroups Association and are non-profit making. The fees are therefore minimal although parents are expected to offer regular help to the group on a rota basis. For this reason and because the sessions tend to be shorter (two to two-and-a-half hours), they are rarely suitable for families where both parents work. Some groups are run almost entirely by volunteer parents, one of whom is qualified, while others employ a teacher or nursery nurse. A volunteer parent can go on to do further training, often in association with the Pre-School Playgroups Association. Places are usually available from three years and given on a first come, first served basis. There is often more than one to choose from in an area and they are held in a variety of places from scout huts to church halls. Some are even held in a spare room of a primary school and form close links with that school, particularly in more rural areas.

Child-minders

Sending your child to a registered child-minder does not, on its own, prepare your child for school. She is not likely to be part of a larger group of children of similar ages nor is she necessarily going to be involved in any learning activities. A child-minder is not a teacher or nursery nurse and is paid to care for your child, not prepare her for school. However, some child-minders are prepared to take your child to and from a nursery or playgroup. This then gives parents a bigger choice of pre-school provision. Make sure when choosing a child-minder that he or she is registered with Social Services.

Finding out what is available

- Contact your local Social Services department to find out about day nurseries. They also keep a register of playgroups and child-minders.
- Private nursery schools also have to be registered with the Social Services so they may have a list. Your local education authority may help. Most are listed in the yellow pages.
- The local education authority will be able to tell you about state nursery schools and how to apply.
- Your health visitor is a good source of information and will certainly know about day nurseries and playgroups. A health visitor or social worker will be able to help you if you think your child qualifies for a priority place at a nursery.
- Look on notice boards in the library, post office and health centre. The library may also keep a register.
- Contact the Pre-School Playgroups Association (or Scottish Pre-School Playgroups Association), London Montessori Centre or the British Association for Early Childhood Education. Addresses and telephone numbers are at the back of the book.

Making your choice

Are you working?

This will obviously be an important factor as you will need to choose a nursery which suits your working hours. You can increase your choice by finding a child-minder who is prepared to take your child to and from nursery. You may want to choose somewhere near your place of work or persuade your company to set up its own nursery by doing a survey of workers to prove the need.

Do you know which school your child will attend?

If you already know which primary school he will be going to, you might choose a nursery or playgroup nearby where your child will make friends who will be going to the same school. Nurseries or playgroups attached or affiliated to the school would obviously be ideal. If your child will be going to a private school, ask the school if it can recommend a suitable nursery.

Is size important?

Not necessarily, although the ratio of staff to children is. According to Social Service recommendations, playgroups should have at least one adult to eight children, including parent volunteers. Nursery schools and classes should have one adult to every 13 children. This is set down by the Department of Education although you may find some private nurseries have more adults. Ask what the ratio is when you visit. If your child is shy, perhaps a small group would suit him better, bearing in mind that it is preparation for school and a class of maybe 30 children.

What qualifications do the leaders have?

A playgroup should include one adult with a playgroup leader's qualification. Nurseries should include a nursery teacher or nursery nurse. If your child is to attend a private nursery with substantial fees, you should expect at least one trained nursery teacher. When you visit, you should ask how long the staff have been there and what experience, as well as qualifications, they have.

What is the equipment and accommodation like?

Make sure that your child will have the space and accommodation for messy activities like painting and sand and water play. Check that equipment is occasionally updated and replaced, that there is a quiet area for books and that the children have the opportunity to play outside.

What is their educational philosophy?

Make sure the aims of the nursery or playgroup match yours. Do you want your child to have some formal education, including specific pre-reading and pre-writing skills? Does your child need a highly structured day or does he respond best to a free play situation? Think about what would suit your child rather than having any set ideas about what he should learn. When you look round playgroups and nurseries, your child may give you an immediate indication of whether he likes it or not so watch for his reaction.

Where do you live?

Your child may find it difficult to cope with a long walk or journey to the group. You need to decide how far you are prepared to travel and look for a group within that distance. Choosing a group nearby means that your child can make friends living close to you who are then likely to attend the same school.

Arrange a visit

You and your child need to visit any groups you are interested in. Try and visit more than one so that you can make direct comparisons.

PREPARE YOUR CHILD FOR SCHOOL

At the visit ask about:	size of group and staff–pupil ratio
	parental involvement
	hours and cost
	waiting list for entry
	age for recommended entry
	arrangements for preparatory visits to a primary school
	policy for behaviour and courtesy
	aims of the group
	staff training and staff turnover
	where most of the children go on to school
	how the sessions are structured
	whether drinks and snacks are provided
	whether trips out are arranged
At the visit note:	your child's reaction
	how the teacher/leader relates to your child
	how the teacher/leader relates to the other children
	the noise level
	the work displayed on the wall. Is it recent?
	the equipment and whether it is appropriate and in reasonable condition
	whether there is an outdoor play area
	the atmosphere – is it calm, homely and reasonably intimate?
	whether staff and pupils seem happy and relaxed
	your gut feeling or intuition

Lost in the pre-school maze? – parents' questions

> ❛ My child will eventually be going to nursery for five mornings a week. This is quite a big step – is there any way I can prepare her for it? ❜

Make sure that your child has visited the nursery at least once and knows what to expect. If you know of any other children going there, invite them to play so that your child sees some familiar faces on the first day. Talk about what is going to happen and get books out of the library to start the conversation off. There are numerous books about going to playgroup or nursery which tell the story of a child's day there. Get your child used to being part of a bigger group of children by taking her to a parent and toddler group. This is where toddlers have the opportunity to play together while parents watch. Ask your health visitor if there are any in your area. Sometimes they are held at the same venue as the playgroup and use some of their equipment. This is ideal, especially if your child will be going on to join the group.

> ❛ How often should my child go to a pre-school group? ❜

This will depend on your circumstances and on the needs of your child. If you are not working, you may be able to start your child with two or three sessions and then build up to five or more sessions as school approaches. In fact, if your time is flexible, you may want to involve your child in other pre-school activities such as mini-gymnastics, dancing or swimming lessons. However, remember that your child needs time to himself as well, both to relax and so that he learns to occupy himself without expecting continuous entertainment. If you are working and your child spends longer sessions at nursery, they should structure the time so that there are

PREPARE YOUR CHILD FOR SCHOOL

quiet listening times or even rest times between the more energetic activities. Remember that your child is bound to feel tired when he first starts a group but this will pass once he has settled into the routine. Allow your child a quiet time when he gets home, perhaps with a high energy snack.

❛ *There are very few playgroups in our area. Could I start my own?* ❜

Yes. Contact the Pre-School Playgroups Association for further advice (the address is at the back of the book). Playgroups must be registered with Social Services, who lay down their particular requirements including the number of children allowed on the premises and how many adults are needed to supervise them. One adult should be qualified; a standard course for playgroup leaders involves 120 hours of study. The venue must be suitable with the necessary fire precautions and first aid equipment, and the group needs insurance for all risks. There is no reason why a small group could not be run in part of your house provided the necessary criteria are met. Parent and toddler groups do not have to be registered as a parent remains present and in charge of his or her own child. A playgroup could be run on the same basis with parents staying and arranging group activities between them.

❛ *How soon should I put my child's name down for nursery?* ❜

As soon as possible. A good private nursery will fill up very quickly and you may need to put her name down soon after she is born. Playgroups may not accept names so early but you will need to enquire when your child is 18 months to two years old. There is nothing to stop you putting your child's name down for more than one nursery although some private nurseries take a deposit which is non-returnable if your child does not go there. There may be no advantage to putting your child's name down early for a state nursery if age is the criteria for selection rather than first come, first served. You need to find out how to register your child from your education authority.

Do not be put off if your child is on a waiting list for a private nursery – yours will not be the only child on more than one list so some may drop out nearer the time of entry. If you do put your child's name down for a nursery very early, keep your ears and eyes open. Nurseries can change if new teachers are employed, and some may close down while new ones will be set up. Keep an open mind and visit again when your child is a little older.

What is a rising fives group?

Some areas provide a playgroup for all children from the age of three until school age while others segregate the older children (those approaching five) for one or two of the sessions. This is usually called a rising fives group. If there is a state nursery school in the area with a rising fives group, it will take those unable to have a nursery place. Some children, of course, go to a combination of groups so that they attend nursery for perhaps three sessions, playgroup for one or two sessions and rising fives for another session, for example.

The difference between a playgroup and a rising fives group is therefore one of age and consequently ability and developmental level. There is a very wide range of ability in a three- to five-year-old group with the older children able to concentrate for longer and tackle more demanding tasks. A rising fives group aims to prepare children for school in a more direct way, encouraging them to sit at a table for paper and pencil tasks for example. The emphasis is still very much on learning through play but this will be more structured.

Another name you may hear is opportunity group. This is essentially a playgroup for children with special needs or learning difficulties. Remember too that some pre-school groups come disguised under different names – anything from 'Little Elves Club' to 'First Steps Group'.

CHAPTER TEN

Ready for the three Rs

Getting your child ready for the three Rs certainly does not mean teaching him the alphabet or how to count up to a hundred. It largely means getting your child enthusiastic and aware of numbers and words. Your child should be starting school with an eagerness to learn, a love of books and confidence in what numbers are all about. Of course, some children may be counting things out, recognising or even writing their name. But remember that children develop at their own rates so do not be tempted to teach your child as much as possible before she starts. In fact, your child will be learning about the three Rs without you even realising it. Every time you read him a story, draw pictures together or go shopping, he is learning something. The following get-ready guides describe some activities you can carry out at home, but remember always to go at your child's own pace.

The ready-to-read guide

Step one: get your child interested in books

This starts almost as soon as your baby can hold a book and probably before she can talk. Make sure that you are not constantly whipping books away from her for fear of getting them torn. Give your child plastic and board books to look at on her own and keep the others for looking at together until she is past the destructive stage. From at least 18 months, you should be reading to your child every day – you do not have to stick to the script, chatting about the pictures or simplifying a repetitive story is fine. Make it a special, quiet time together with your child so that you both look forward to it. Join the library as early as possible and let your child have the fun of choosing at least some of the books. Make sure she sees you choosing yours too and let her see *you* reading at home with obvious enjoyment. If your child likes a particular television programme or if she is fond of animals, tractors or teddies for example, choose books to compliment and reinforce her interests. Continue to encourage a love of books after she has started school and carry on reading to her even after she has started to read herself.

Step two: tell stories together

Your child needs to be able to use and understand the words that she will be learning to read later. She needs to enjoy listening to stories and be able to tell stories of her own. When you read to your child, talk about the pictures and what is happening in the story. Ask her to find things in the picture and see if she can guess what is going to happen next. Get her to relate a familiar story to you by looking at the pictures and do not interrupt when you hear her telling stories to her dolls and teddies. Build up her vocabulary by talking all the time, pointing things out when you are out and about as well as looking at pictures in books.

Step three: teach your child the meaning of written words

When you are reading to your child, you can run your finger underneath the words as you do. You can explain that these words tell you what to say as you tell the story. Draw his attention to the written words around your home or out in the streets – shop names, signposts, cereal packets and so on. The word your child will be most interested in is his name so write it on books, on his cup and on the bedroom door. You will soon find that your child runs his own finger under a word and 'reads' it by making a guess, sometimes lucky. At this point, you can start sticking labels on items around the house using large, clear print and lower case (i.e. not capitals) letters. Stick the word 'door' on the door, 'chair' on the chair and so on.

Step four: make your own book

Make a scrap book together, starting with a picture of your child on the first page. Write her name underneath and then let your child stick in pictures of other people in the family. Start by writing single words underneath each picture but later you could turn the book into something more like a diary. Let your child draw a picture of what you did one day, sticking in any relevant items such as entrance tickets or pressed leaves. Then decide together what to write underneath. Stick to a simple sentence such as 'We went for a picnic' or 'I went to play with Sarah'.

Step five: play matching games

Before reading stories, your child needs to know how to match words – perhaps by finding two words the same in a game. However, you will need to work towards this skill with other games. Start by playing picture lotto with your two- or three-year-old. This is a game of small pictures which match on to a board of six to nine identical pictures. You can make your own version by cutting out pictures from two identical catalogues. Now see if your child can match shapes – again you can make your own picture pairs or picture lotto game. Start with shapes which look very different from each other, perhaps circles, squares, straight lines and stars. Gradually introduce other more similar shapes such as squares and rectangles, circles and ovals. You can even use individual letters, again starting with those which look most different from each other, such as 'o', 'v', 'm' and 's' rather than 'p', 'b', 'q' and 'd'. Now go back to your scrap book where you have stuck in and labelled pictures of the family. Write out the words on individual cards and see if your child can match these with the words written in the book.

Step six: play memory games

When your child learns to read, she will need to remember shapes of words. Playing visual memory games will help her work towards this skill. Start with a simple hiding game – get your child to hide four or five objects around the room and then see if she can remember where they are. Then try Kim's game – put a number of items on a tray and take one away while your child closes her eyes. She then has to tell you which one is missing. Make this more difficult by filling the tray with an increasing number of items, remove the lot and see how many she can remember. As your child approaches school age, try making a very simple picture or shape out of sticker shapes or coloured bricks. Let your child study it, then cover it up and see if she can make one exactly the same. As she gets more proficient at this game, gradually add more detail. If your child is ready, take the labels off the furniture and see if she can remember which one goes where. When she can do this she really is reading.

Step seven: make her aware of letters

Learning the alphabet off by heart is not as useful as you may think. It is far better for your child to develop an awareness of the *sounds* letters make. So when you refer to the letters, use the sounds they make and not the names of the letters so that 'g' is not 'gee' but 'g' on its own. Be careful not to emphasise the vowel sound that follows. Make or buy an alphabet book or alphabet frieze so that she can learn that 'a' is for 'apple', 'b' is for 'ball', etc. What you are aiming for is for your child to be able to hear the sound which starts a word. So take away the visual clues and just get her to listen. When you say 'apple', 'alligator' or 'ant', she has to tell you that they begin with 'a'. She will probably find this difficult at first so over-emphasise the first sound by saying 'a-pple' (with a slight pause after the 'a' sound). Now see if she can think of anything beginning with 'a', 'b', 'c', etc, using the sound, not the name of the letter. If she still finds this activity difficult try getting her used to listening with some other activities. You could try recording sounds around the house such as the tap running or the door banging and see if your child can identify them. Or try some of the other listening activities outlined in chapter 6. Once she can hear the letters at the beginnings of words, point out their shapes in the alphabet book or use the magnetic letters which stick to the fridge.

Step eight: read together

Start by letting your child join in with the repetitive lines in a story – 'Run, run as fast as you can and you can't catch me I'm the gingerbread man' or 'I'll huff and I'll puff and I'll blow your house down' for example. Run your finger under the words as you say them together. Now, when you are reading to your child, spend more time drawing his attention to the text. You can point out any familiar words that come up or words that start with the same sound as his name. It is unlikely that you will want to start with a reading scheme as such. Building up his awareness, enthusiasm and the beginnings of word recognition is far more important. However, if you really feel that your child is ready, you could try one of the parent–child schemes available in most book shops. The most useful type at this stage would be books which have a story for you to read on one page and a few key words for your child to have a go at on the opposite page. Never push your child into doing something she is not ready for or interested in. Your child will do far better if she starts school eager to learn and enthusiastic about books.

The ready-to-write guide

Step one: getting interested and aware

First your child needs to be keen on using pencils, crayons, felt pens and paint brushes – in fact anything which makes a mark on the paper. Paint brushes are probably the easiest to start with as they are easy to wield and give a pleasing result however they are held. Praise all your child's efforts and do not worry if her drawing does not look like anything yet. Draw her attention to any writing which you have done, whether it is a letter to Grandma, a shopping list or a note to the milkman. This will show her how useful writing is and if she watches you actually doing it, she will learn that it goes from left to right and from the top of the page to the bottom. Soon she will be doing her own pretend writing – rows and rows of scribble – and you'll know her enthusiasm for writing has started.

Step two: developing good hand control

Your child will need good hand control before he will be able to make a pencil do what he wants. Playing with play-dough or Plasticine will help to develop the appropriate muscles. Then try tasks involving eye–hand co-ordination such as cutting round pictures with scissors and threading beads, dried macaroni or cut-up straws. Sewing cards can be made by drawing a simple outline of an animal or object on to a thick piece of card. Using a knitting needle, make holes around the outline about two centimetres apart. Now show your child how to sew with wool and a darning needle. A safe plastic child's sewing needle would be even better.

Step three: developing pencil control

Start by ensuring that she is holding her pencil correctly. By three years, she should be able to hold a pencil in her preferred hand, near the bottom with a tripod grip (using tips of thumb and fingers).

For a while, she may automatically pick up the pencil in her palm so put the pencil in the correct position for her until it becomes automatic. Encourage her to do free drawing but at the same time see if she can try some more specific tasks requiring greater pencil control. Using two parallel lines, draw a road for your child to pencil between using a straight line from left to right. Make it more interesting by drawing a mouse at one end and a piece of cheese at the other or a car and garage. Then you can make a story out of it. Play a beetle game where you start with a body and add an item – legs, feelers, head, etc – depending on what number is thrown on the dice. Draw faces or animals and ask your child to draw in the eyes, nose, mouth or ears. Make some dot-to-dot outlines for your child to draw around and encourage her to colour pictures in, which is a very good activity for developing pencil control.

Step four: writing on top

Start by encouraging your child to trace simple pictures or go over shapes or pictures you have already drawn using a felt pen or paint brush. Once she can do this, you can see if she can go over the top of some of the easiest letters with a pencil – 'o', 'v' and 'c' for example. You draw your version in a light yellow crayon so that her pencil version on the top stands out well. Work towards your child being able to write on top of her own name – she will certainly be delighted with this achievement.

Step five: copying shapes and letters

See if your child can copy simple shapes – a square, a circle and a triangle. Once he has mastered this, he could try copying an 'o', a 'v' and then some of the other easier letters. When he can do enough, make words out of the letters which he can copy, but always accompany the word with a picture which you or he can draw. This makes it more meaningful. Many children are not up to copy writing until after they have started school so go slowly and carefully at your child's own pace. It should always be enjoyable and fun for both of you.

Step six: writing his name

The most satisfying word your child can learn to write is his name, even though other words may be easier. Again, many children will not be able to write their names when they start school and a lot will depend on the letters involved. This is where you wished you had called him Tim instead of Christopher! If your child can copy his name on top or underneath your writing, see if he can put card or magnetic letters in the right order (name puzzles are quite useful at this stage). Once he has mastered this, see if he can either start or finish his name with you writing the most difficult letters. Gradually help him write more of the letters until he can do the whole word. But even if your child can only do the first letter of his name, praise his efforts and encourage him to 'initial' all his pictures and paintings.

The ready-for-maths guide

Step one: sorting and matching

The first skill you can help your child with is matching things together and sorting items into groups. Play picture and colour matching games such as lotto or dominoes to start with. Once your child can do this, try a children's version of number dominoes. Use everyday situations to get your child to sort and match. For example, when you are sorting out the washing, get her to match up all the socks and sort the shirts into colours. When you go shopping, see if she can find all the ten pence pieces in your purse and when you put the shopping away, ask her to sort out all the things you eat for breakfast and all the things you eat for tea. Talk about 'same' and 'different' in all sorts of situations, from car spotting on a journey to browsing round clothes shops.

Step two: size and amount

Your child needs to have a concept of size and quantity before he can really grasp the meaning behind numbers. Let him discover some things for himself by experimenting with different sized bottles in the bath or by tackling jigsaw puzzles. Talk about big and little things when you are dishing up food or sorting the washing. Make 'big' and 'little' scrap books where your child sticks pictures of little things into the 'little' book and pictures of things bigger than, say, a chair into the 'big' book. But always relate the pictures to the real thing so that he can *see* that a chair is bigger than a pencil. If he finds this difficult, play teddy bears' picnics. Talk about giving the *big* teddies the *most* food and putting *more* drink into the *big* cups. Other concepts to introduce are long and short, fat and thin and tall and short, to start comparing the sizes and shapes of everyone in the family, including all the pets.

Step three: shapes and patterns

Make a domino or picture lotto game using shapes. Simply draw the shapes on to each lotto board and have about six matching shapes to put on top. Start with circles, squares and triangles and when your child can recognise and identify those, introduce rectangles, ovals and diamonds. Remember though that many children will only know the names for a circle and square when they start school so take it slowly. Play an I spy game – perhaps on a car journey – where you have to spot anything square, round or triangular. Cut potato halves into different shapes, dip them in paint and make a pattern with them. If you start off a line pattern of circle, square, circle, square, see if your child can carry on the sequence. Now try a sequence of three.

Step four: counting

Most children learn to count up to at least ten before they start school. This is not terribly useful on its own – it is far more useful if your child can count out three pieces of fruit for herself and three for her sister. Certainly teach your child to count to ten by rote – there are plenty of songs and rhymes to help you with this such as '1 2 3 4 5, once I caught a fish alive'. Spend some time, though, making the counting more meaningful. Forget about the written numbers to start with – just spend time helping your child count things, whether people, toys, apples or fingers. Start with concrete items and then move on to counting pictures in a number book. Hold your child's hand or finger as she touches each item, counting with her as you do. Start with just three things and when she can do that herself, without counting the same item twice, move on to four, then five and so on. Try and use natural situations to make it more meaningful and interesting. Perhaps you could be counting out spoons to put on the dinner table or sweets to share out.

Step five: recognising written numbers

Once your child has started to count things out meaningfully, you can introduce him to the written numbers. A number book or wall frieze is ideal for this. Choose a book where your child can count the items and then relate his total to the written number on that page. He will soon start to recognise some of the numbers but remember that he does not need to know them all before starting school. So just go at your child's pace, responding to his interest rather than your desire to teach him. Sometimes your child's interest can be maintained by looking for numbers while you are out and about. You can look for numbers on houses, birthday cards, cars and signposts for instance. If he is able to copy the easiest ones such as 1 and 7, do encourage him but always draw that number of items next to it and keep numbers meaningful. Play games with a die – eventually your child will not need to count the dots every time. Write the numbers up to 5 on individual cards or use magnetic numbers on the fridge and see if your child can put them in the right order. Then try with numbers up to 10.

Step six: more or less

This is really the beginning of adding up and taking away. When you give your child, say, five pieces of apple, make it into a game by getting her to count how many she has got left after she has eaten one. Now do it the other way round, giving her one piece at a time with your child counting to see how many she has every time you give her another. Soon she may even be able to predict how many there will be without counting them all out every time. There are numerous counting songs which either keep adding one on or taking one away. Try 'Ten green bottles', 'Ten men went to mow' or 'Five little ducks went swimming one day', for example. You could buy a tape of number songs or else record yourselves singing them. When your child is familiar with the songs, stop the tape occasionally and see if she can remember which number comes next.

On the write track? – parents' questions

> ❛ I think my four-year-old may be dyslexic. He writes many of his letters and numbers back to front. ❜

All children go through a stage of letter reversal while they are learning to write so it is not likely to be a symptom of dyslexia on its own. Dyslexia is a specific learning difficulty with reading and writing so letter reversal is only really relevant if the child is doing it long after he should be past that stage (seven or eight in some cases). Dyslexia cannot therefore be diagnosed very easily in pre-school children as you would not yet be expecting them to be reading and writing. Later, not only will letters be written back to front but word order will be disrupted, letters within words are likely to be in the wrong order and writing may even run from right to left. However, if your child has a mixed laterality (has not decided whether he is right- or left-handed), is very hyperactive or has a severe speech problem, do mention it to the teacher so that progress can be monitored carefully as your child learns to read and write.

(*My child is left-handed. Will the teacher know what to do?*)

As one in ten children are left-handed, your child's teacher will have plenty of experience in teaching left-handers and your child is unlikely to be the only one in the class. Writing is not easy for left-handers because we write from left to right. A left-handed person tends to cover up what has been written and a slightly different movement of the hand is involved. Show your child how to grip the pencil by demonstrating with *your* left hand (just the grip, you do not have to write anything if you are right-handed). Get her to hold the pencil a little further from the end than a right-hander and position the paper at an angle so that she can see what she has just written or copied.

(*My child can trace some words but does it matter how exactly she does this?*)

Yes. Try to encourage your child to write letters correctly even at the tracing stage. By noting how *you* write letters, you can work out the starting point for each letter and which direction the pencil goes in. For some letters, of course, the pencil goes over part of the letter twice. Hold your child's hand as he writes to encourage correct formation. If he finds this difficult, make some giant letters out of cardboard and practice going over them (by the correct route) with your finger. Once your child gets the idea, let her have a go on her own but put a dot on the starting point for each letter to begin with. Remember though, the key is to *encourage* correct letter formation not to insist on it absolutely. If your child has not yet started school, he is unlikely to be perfect at this skill so praise all his efforts even if mistakes are made. You can do games and activities to encourage the correct form but if he manages to write his name,

PREPARE YOUR CHILD FOR SCHOOL

albeit with some letters written awkwardly from bottom to top, concentrate on praising rather than criticising or correcting.

❝ *My child prefers comics to books. Should I discourage him?* **❞**

No. In the early stages it is important to follow your child's interest and if he likes comics then look at these together, applying the same principles outlined for sharing books. Remember as well that pre-school comics have a very high educational value and are certainly not to be sneered at. Once your child has started school, he should develop some interest in books, though comics do not have to be given up. See if a comic or magazine throws up any topic which particularly interests him and choose books which follow this interest up. He may be following your example of reading more comics (magazines and newspapers) than books. So make sure he sees *you* taking books out of the library and reading for pleasure. However, do carry on keeping a comic or magazine for your child alongside yours on the coffee table or in the magazine rack, whatever his age.

❝ *My child can hold a thick felt pen very well but finds an ordinary pencil difficult.* **❞**

Let your child use whatever she chooses for drawing but encourage the use of a pencil for copying shapes and letters. You can buy pencil grips which fit onto the end where your child's fingers go. Alternatively, you could put several layers of sticky tape around the appropriate place to encourage your child to grip the right place and to make gripping slightly easier by increasing the width of the pencil.

CHAPTER ELEVEN

Which school?

Your child has a right to education from the age of five, although many children start school slightly earlier than this. You will live in a catchment area of a particular primary school and your child is normally entitled to a place there. However, provided there is a place available, you have the right to choose any school even if it is outside your catchment area. Parents also have the option of paying to send their child to a private school or of educating their child at home. Whichever type of school you choose, you need to give it some thought very early. If you decide to move house, even if your child is still a toddler, you should find out from the local education authority which school's catchment area you would be in. Some people even move to be in a particular catchment area. If you choose to educate your child privately, you need to be prepared even earlier as most will take children on a first come, first served basis. Whatever your choice and wherever you live, you need to look round your local school and any others you are interested in before applying for a place. After all, you will want to make the right choice before your child is five because once she has started school, settled in and made friends, moving schools could be difficult and unsettling.

PREPARE YOUR CHILD FOR SCHOOL

How to choose a state primary school

- Firstly, you need to know what is available. If you have lived in the area a long time, you will probably already know. If not, you can obtain a list from your local education authority.
- You then need to decide how far it is reasonable to travel. If you live in a rural area, there may only be one choice within a reasonable distance anyway.
- You may end up with a list of three or four schools you want to know more about. Arrange a visit to all of them so that you can make direct comparisons. Have a list of questions to ask each head teacher and get a prospectus from each school.
- Listen to what other parents say. However, make sure they are parents with children currently at the school. Information about schools quickly becomes out of date, particularly if there has been a change of head teacher.
- Find out if the school has any events coming up such as a jumble sale which is open to the public. Go along to this – although you will not see the school at work, it will give you a chance to take note of the facilities.

The visit

Few primary schools can show all the potential parents around individually. You are more likely to attend an open day or look round in small groups. Make the most of this by having questions prepared and a list of what you want to look out for. Parents have their own ideas of what sort of school they want, but most want something to help their child reach his potential in all areas of the curriculum. Some prefer a more relaxed atmosphere while others feel a more formal old-fashioned approach would best suit their child. Whatever your views you need to notice or ask about the following:

Checklist of questions when visiting a school

Class size

How big are existing classes? What is the maximum intake and what intake is expected for your child's year? Are the classes divided into year groups or are they mainly composite classes (made up of more than one age group)?

The teachers

Have they been in the school for a long time or is there a big turnover of staff? Do they seem to relate well to the children? How do they react to your child as you look around?

The head teacher

Many people say that a good head teacher makes a good school. Does she seem to know all the names of the children in the school? Do they like her?

The children

Do they seem busy, happy, relaxed and confident?

The atmosphere

Is it noisy? Is it relaxed? Is it conducive to work without being too formal? Is there enough room for work and play?

The equipment

Is there a computer in each classroom or are there plans to have one? Are there plenty of books in good condition? Is there up-to-date work on display?

Discipline

What is the school's policy on this? Does it encourage good manners? Do the children seem polite and courteous?

Teaching methods

Do the teachers give clear answers when you ask what methods they use to teach reading, writing and maths? Are they flexible in their approach to reading? Do the books in the scheme look up to date, fun and interesting?

Provision for slow or fast learners

Is there a learning support system for children who struggle to keep up? Are bright children allowed to go on ahead with workbooks and reading books or does the teacher try and keep all the children at the same level?

Other activities and parental involvement

Are there any after-school clubs or activities, indicating a high level of teacher commitment? Are parents involved with these and any other school activities? Are imaginative outings organised each term? Is there an active Parent–teacher Association?

Non-teaching staff

Are there any other members of staff employed to help the infant classes? Or are parents involved?

Settling in

What visits are arranged for children about to start school? What arrangements are made to help the new starters settle in?

Uniform

Is it mandatory? If not, how many children wear it?

Progress

How are parents informed of progress? Are there frequent parents' evenings? Are reports sent home at least once a year, preferably every term? Can you arrange to see the teacher or head at any time?

Future plans

Are there any changes planned for the near future including staff changes, curriculum changes or new buildings?

Applying for a place

You may be asked to fill in an application form when you visit the school. Alternatively, your local education authority will provide a form on which you can put your choices, usually in order of preference. Your local education authority will tell you the last date for applications, normally about a year in advance of school entry. If you live in the catchment area of the school you want, then there should be no problem getting a place. If you prefer schools outside your catchment area, then apply for more than one as you cannot assume there will be a place at the school of your choice. A school does not have to take your child if it is full once the local children have had their places allocated. You will not be told if your child has a place until about half a term before the school entry date so have an alternative lined up. If you do not get a place at the school of your choice, ask to be kept on the waiting list as some children may not accept their places. You can even consider changing schools when your child is seven as places sometimes become available if children leave to go to a private preparatory school.

How to appeal

If the school does turn your child down, you will be told how to appeal. This is worth doing as many appeals are successful. Appealing involves writing to say why you prefer that school and later answering questions at the appeal itself. Make sure your reasons are clear – just saying that one school is better than the other is not going to get you very far. Good reasons are:

Convenience	The school may be near your work or home.
Family links	Brothers or sisters already go there (this should make you a priority). Other family links.
Other links	If your child has attended a nursery or playgroup where most of the children go on to the school of your choice.
Religion	The school has a particular religious tradition. Or perhaps you want your child to go to a non-church school.
Size	You feel a smaller (or bigger) school would suit your child better. Perhaps he has a particular problem such as a physical difficulty, a speech or language delay or fluctuating hearing loss and a smaller school would be more suitable.
Teaching methods	Having visited the schools in the area (essential before appealing), you have a strong preference for the methods of one school. Or perhaps it specialises in a particular area such as art, music or sport.

Remember to attend the appeal hearing and write down what you want to say. Letters from a professional such as a doctor, playgroup leader, speech and language therapist or social worker can be used to support your arguments.

How to choose a private school

Private schools are also known as independent schools and, for older children, public schools. They can be co-educational (mixed) or single sex and are likely to have smaller classes than state-run primary schools. Generally, they take children on a first come, first served basis and for a popular school you will need to put down your child's name soon after he is born. However, most schools will look at your child as school age approaches and he may be observed or tested informally before a place is offered. If you have put your child's name down early, you will want to look round the school once your child is older and ask similar questions to those you ask at a state primary school. You may want to look round more than one private school, and your local primary, so you can make some direct comparisons. You need to do the following when you make your choice:

- Find out what is available in your area by contacting the Independent Schools Information Service (ISIS) – the address is at the back of the book. Your library may also have copies of the Independent Schools Year Book or Preparatory School Year Book. The yellow pages is another source of information.
- Send for a prospectus and details of fees from each school.
- Visit any you are interested in and if you are still keen, ask for an application form there and then. You may need to pay a small registration fee. Re-visit the school as school age approaches.
- Talk to other parents with children at the school.
- Ask additional questions applicable to private schools. This will include asking whether the school pays attention to the National Curriculum (they do not have to), uniform details, likely changes in fees and additional costs for extra items such

as music lessons. If it is a preparatory (prep) school (up to 11-
or 13-year-olds), you will also want to know which school the
children usually go on to next.

Teaching your child at home

The law states that your child has to receive a full-time education
from the age of five, not that she should go to school. You are
therefore entitled to educate your child at home if you choose. This
is done by a small minority of parents, sometimes right from the
start, because they feel it would suit the family better, or else after
their child has had a bad school experience. If you feel that this is
a viable option for your family, you need to do the following:

- Think very carefully. This is a very big decision to make and
  will involve full-time commitment from at least one parent.
- Contact Education Otherwise, an advisory and support group
  for parents who choose to educate their children at home (its
  address is at the back of the book).
- Contact your local education authority and inform it of your
  intention. It will send an inspector round to discuss your plans.
  You do not need to be trained to teach your child but you
  must convince the education authorities that you know what
  you are doing. In fact, most education authorities are very
  supportive.
- Contact your local school and discuss with it and the education
  authority the possibility of your child attending school for
  social activities or play time.
- Buy the books and equipment you need.

The education authority has to provide your child with a place if
you want it, even if he has spent the first few years being educated
at home.

Making the choice – your questions answered

❝ *I am not quite sure at what age my child will start school. Some children seem to start at four and others at five.* ❞

Legally, your child has to start school at the beginning of the term which follows her fifth birthday. However, in most areas you are likely to be offered a place before that, usually for the term before her fifth birthday. Not all schools have a termly intake, some have an annual intake and some a twice-yearly intake. The variation will be from area to area, not from school to school as it will depend on the policy of the local education authority. If you are offered an early place, you do not have to accept it – you can wait until your child is of statutory school age. If you feel that your child is exceptionally bright and you want her to start school even earlier than the education authority is offering, you can write to the authority and the school with your reasons. However, it is unlikely that your child would be offered a very early place. Do remember that your child has to be emotionally and socially ready for school, not just intellectually.

❝ *What is the difference between infant and junior schools, primary and middle schools, and reception and first year classes?* ❞

A primary school is for children aged five (or rising five) to 11 years. In some areas, there are separate infant schools (five to seven years) and junior schools (seven to 11 years). Or there may be separate first schools (five to eight or nine years) and middle schools (eight or nine years to 12 or 13 years). Quite often, although the schools are treated as separate with their own head teachers, they are on the same site or even within the same building. Whatever the geography, the infant or first schools have a close affiliation with the

PREPARE YOUR CHILD FOR SCHOOL

junior or middle schools and it is expected that children will automatically move from one to the other.

At the end of the primary years, children move on to the local secondary school which will normally have an intake from several primary schools. You may want to take the secondary school into account when you choose your child's primary school.

Some schools call the very first class the reception class, which is then followed by year one, year two and so on. Children in other schools, particularly in Scotland, go straight into Primary One and move up from there.

In the private sector, schools are called independent schools. A preparatory school (prep school) is an independent school for children aged seven or eight up to 11 or 13 years. A pre-prep school is an independent school for children aged two to four up to seven to eight years old and may be part of a bigger school.

❜ What is a church school? If this is the nearest primary to where we live, does my child have a right to a place? ❝

Church schools are voluntary-aided schools, usually partly funded by a trust or religious denomination. The governors are therefore able to decide their own admission criteria. Priority will be given to church-goers and then the children living nearby, although they can refuse to give a place because of lack of religious commitment whether they are full or not. The school may check on your church attendance record so if you are keen to get a place and have an affiliation with an appropriate church, you may like to enclose a letter from your minister or priest with your application. You are not expected to pay fees at a voluntary-aided school and your child should follow the same curriculum as other schools. However, there is likely to be a greater emphasis on religious education and the children's moral development.

❜ We are about to move to a different area. How do I go about choosing a new school for my child? ❝

WHICH SCHOOL?

You may not have any choice about when you move but as far as possible, it is better to move at the start of an academic year or at least the beginning of a term. You really need to arrange a place in the new school before withdrawing from the old one. You then need to inform your child's current head teacher that he is leaving and pass on the name of your child's new school so that records can be forwarded.

When choosing a school in a new area, the same criteria apply whatever your child's age. You can state a preference and if your child is refused a place, you should appeal in the usual way. Other people move area too so do apply to popular schools which are said to be full – there may be a place in your child's year group. The difficulty with moving area is that you know nothing about the schools there except what you find out as you look round. Try to talk to parents collecting their children from school to get some parental viewpoints. If you or your partner will be starting a new job, you could ask your new employers if they can put you in touch with someone in the know about primary schools in the area. Also, find out if there is a local branch of the Campaign for the Advancement of State Education or the National Confederation of Parent–teacher Associations who may be able to help (their addresses are at the back of the book).

> ❝ What is an open-plan school? My child is easily
> distracted and I would prefer her to attend a more
> traditional school. ❞

Some modern-built primary schools are built in an open-plan system. This means that although there are separate class areas, there are no separate class *rooms* with doors that shut and keep each class completely separate from the rest of the school. Children have a greater sense of freedom in an open-plan school and often feel more relaxed. They learn not to be distracted by the next class, which they will be able to see and even hear. Most open-plan schools do have quiet rooms for things like music or learning support (remedial teaching). It could be that all the schools in your area

PREPARE YOUR CHILD FOR SCHOOL

are open-plan, in which case there will be little choice. However, if there is a variation in your area, you could apply for a school which is not open-plan giving the reason as your child's poor attention. However, do look round each school, note how well the children concentrate in an open-plan situation and ask the teacher for her views on how they would help a child with poor listening skills.

CHAPTER TWELVE

Ready or not?

As the first term approaches, some parents will question whether their child is ready for school either emotionally, socially, developmentally or intellectually. Other parents will just know their child is ready and have no fears or reservations about his ability to cope. The children themselves may have their own fears about school though some will look forward to it with bags of confidence and enthusiasm. Children of this age vary enormously, not only in personality but in development and maturation too. Some already have developed good fine motor skills and speech for example, while others still hold a pencil awkwardly and mispronounce a few sounds. This difference in maturation does not necessarily mean a difference in intelligence or even in the ability to cope with school. The checklist in chapter 1 indicates the sort of tasks your child should be able to manage before school age but this is only a rough guide. There is a huge range of what is normal at this age and there is no need to worry if your child has a particular weakness in one area. However, some parents may want to seek the advice of an appropriate professional if they have particular concerns about their child.

It could be the case that a child is ready for school but that the timing is not quite right. Starting school is a major change for any child and if it coincides with another major change such as the arrival of a new baby in the family, you may want to delay entry by a term so that your child does not have too many changes at once. In the case of a new baby brother or sister, you will not want your older child to feel pushed out in any way. Remember, your child does not have to start school until she is five.

Who are the professionals?

The health visitor's pre-school screening check

In most areas your health visitor will have a final look at your child to check that she is ready for school. She will then send on her health record card to the school with any relevant details from the check added. Your health visitor will have carried out screening tests at about eight or nine months, 18 months and three years (exact ages vary from area to area) and the check during the six months or so before school entry is to ensure that development is still progressing. Any major problems such as a physical difficulty, eye defect or delayed speech development should have been diagnosed as a result of one of the earlier assessments. The final pre-school check is more informal but does give you the chance to discuss any unresolved problems such as bed wetting. The health visitor will note your child's development of fine motor skills including drawing, gross motor skills and co-ordination, social skills and communication. She will weigh and measure your child and discuss starting school with you, answering any questions you have. If there are any specific problems, the health visitor will refer your child to the necessary professional whether it is an orthoptist for an eye test or a speech and language therapist for a communication assessment.

Clinical medical officer

If your child shows any delay or difficulty in his development, your health visitor may refer your child to a specialist doctor (a clinical medical officer or paediatrician) for a more in-depth developmental assessment. Your child could have a specific difficulty or a more global delay. The doctor will give you the appropriate advice and refer your child on for any further treatment.

Educational psychologist

Your health visitor will also refer your child to an educational psychologist if she feels he may have any difficulty coping at school. The educational psychologist will talk to you and your child and observe him as well as carry out some more formal tests. She will want to liaise with the school and keep checking progress as well as give you some initial advice on how best to help your child. The educational psychologist may need to recommend learning support (remedial teaching) if your child has real difficulty but this is unlikely to be arranged when your child first starts school. In extreme cases, where a child has severe difficulties which are likely to be long lasting, she may suggest your child has a statement. This statement outlines your child's special educational needs.

Statements

Children with an obvious disability, for example if they are deaf or have severe learning difficulties, have a special educational need. The parents will have known this for some time. However there are also children who have less severe difficulties and are diagnosed much later as having a special or specific educational need. All these children should have a full assessment and a statement which describes what their needs are. Parents are involved in all stages of preparing the statement, which must involve educational, medical and psychological advice. Some children in this category need to attend a special school and are likely to remain there for the whole of their education. Other children attend a special unit with the aim of gradually integrating back into mainstream education. And others may have their needs met in an ordinary school.

Problems affecting school entry

Physical difficulties

If your child has a profound physical difficulty such as severe cerebral palsy, deafness or blindness then a special school may suit your child's needs best. However, the 1981 Education Act says that a local education authority should meet a parent's request for a child with special needs to be educated in the local school provided certain conditions are met. Firstly, the child's needs must be met adequately in the local school. Secondly, the education of other children in the school must not be damaged and thirdly, the decision must be compatible with the efficient use of resources. If, for example, your child is in a wheelchair then 'normal' education may be appropriate if there are no access problems, if the child does not need intensive physiotherapy with specialist equipment on site and if the child does not also have severe learning or behavioural difficulties which will disrupt the class and take up too large a proportion of teacher time.

Learning difficulties

Again, if your child has severe learning difficulties, her needs may be best met in a special school or unit. However, many children have far more temporary learning difficulties – perhaps they are slow in learning to read and write, for example. These children are often best helped by having additional teaching within their local school. This is known as learning support (it used to be called remedial teaching). It is often difficult to predict whether your child is likely to have any learning difficulties. However, if he is clearly struggling with the tasks at nursery or playgroup, then you may want some advice before he starts school.

Emotional difficulties

Some children have severe emotional or behavioural difficulties which can clearly affect their progress at school. You can ask your health visitor to refer your child to the psychological service (still called child guidance in some areas), which will offer you advice. In many parts of the country, either Social Services or the psychological service can arrange family therapy to help with emotional or behavioural problems. Remember that anxiety or emotional problems can manifest themselves in a physical way such as bedwetting.

If your child is not ready

If you feel that your child is not ready, you will need to discuss this with the school, although hopefully any major difficulties would have been identified a lot earlier. Your child's pre-school teacher and future school teacher will be happy to discuss any worries you may have. It could be that they disagree with you and feel that starting school in itself will help your child mature and develop. However, if your child has a more severe delay in development or a specific difficulty, you may need a referral to a specialist. You will then get the appropriate advice, which may be to delay school entry by a term. This would allow your child to receive the necessary help and to mature a little more before school entry. Remember, your child does not *have* to start school until he is five and in some cases this is more appropriate. Schools and specialists are unlikely to stop your child from starting school but will advise you about the appropriate time to start (or about attending a special school or unit). You will have the opportunity to put your views and ask questions whenever a decision is made about your child's education.

The role of the school

The school itself usually plays some part both in preparing your child for school and in ensuring that your child is ready. Most schools arrange for children to visit the school at least once before starting. This has the dual purpose of familiarising the children with the school and the teachers, and of allowing the teachers to observe and get to know the children. Some teachers also visit the new entrants at their playgroup or nursery to observe them in a familiar and relaxed setting. They can also take this opportunity to chat informally to playgroup leaders and nursery teachers.

Most schools also give you written information before your child starts. Apart from the school prospectus, you may get an induction booklet with details about starting school. This should tell you the names of the staff (particularly your child's teacher), exactly when school starts, what to take on the first day, uniform details and what to do if you have any queries. Some booklets go further, advising about preparing your child for school and discussing likely problems during the first weeks such as excessive tiredness.

Are you ready?

Although the focus is very much on your child and her readiness for school, the change in your child's life will affect the whole family, especially if there is a younger child at home or if you have been at home caring for the child about to start school. Many parents become anxious about their child starting school, not just because they are worried about how *she* will cope but because they are worried about how *they* will cope. As your child is likely to respond to any anxiety or tension that you have, try to relax and stop worrying by doing the following:

Prepare *yourself* for school!

- Find out as much as possible about the school and what your child will be doing during her first weeks.
- When you meet your child's new teacher, discuss any worries that you have.
- Make sure that *you* are used to being apart from your child.
- Make sure that you have plans for yourself if this is your last child to start school and you have not been working. Perhaps you want to return to work or take up a new interest.
- Make your plans in advance. Do not wait until your child is at school to start applying for jobs or to get involved with something new. These things take time to organise, so get the ball rolling ahead of the first school day.
- Have very specific plans for the first day or you could spend all day worrying about your child and wondering what she is doing. Get together with parents in the same situation.
- For your own peace of mind, make sure that the school has your telephone number (they should have organised this in advance) and the number of where you will be on day one.
- If you have another child at home, plan a treat or a day out as the younger child will miss her older brother or sister. However, do not make a big thing of this or your older child may not want to go to school for fear of missing something.
- If you have been working and your child was cared for by someone else most days, then the change to your

PREPARE YOUR CHILD FOR SCHOOL

life style could be minimal. Remember though, that it *is* a big change for your child so get her prepared in the usual way.

- Talk to other parents who went through it all last year, they will know how you feel.
- Do not try and cover up any difficulty your child has. If he still wets himself occasionally, is reluctant to communicate or clings on to you whenever you leave him, tell the teacher so that she can help him. She will also reassure you. You will probably find that you feel less anxious once the school is aware of any difficulties.
- Do not worry if it has been recommended that your child's school entry is delayed. If a child starts school too soon, it could put him off for a long time.

Parents and teachers say . . .

❝ We had an induction booklet from the school with a lot of practical advice. It was mostly common sense but was also very reassuring. I knew Heather was ready for school as she could already do all the things they suggested helping with, such as dressing herself and doing her shoes up. ❞

Linda Miles, Kingswells

❝ Not having had any tears from my new arrivals that first morning, I was amused when tears eventually came from one boy when his Mum arrived to take him home for lunch. He didn't want to go home! He must have been ready for school. ❞

Sheila Reidford, infant teacher, Monymusk

❝ Parents can do a lot to prepare their child for school.

READY OR NOT?

They can develop his independence, confidence and self-esteem. They can give him a positive attitude to school through their own positive handling of the child. And they can reassure, listen to and support their child.

Nursery teacher, Westhill

Victoria kept asking to go to school on Saturday and Sunday. Despite her nursery experience, visits to the school and preparation from me, nobody had told her that she would get two days off each week!

Colin Watson, Aberdeen

Parents should choose a good and productive nursery or pre-school group. They should encourage interaction with children who may be going to a new school with them. They should talk to their child about school and have a positive and encouraging outlook on school themselves. Negative feelings can be passed on to the child which can then unsettle them.

Noreen Jones, nursery teacher, Aberdeen

CHAPTER THIRTEEN

Starting school – the first term

The first day at school is a big step, not only for your child but for you and the rest of the family. It is therefore all too easy to have a big build up, sometimes lasting many months, which can often do more harm than good. Big build ups can create either acute anxiety or immense over-excitement in your child as the event draws nearer. On the other hand, the first day certainly should not arrive virtually unannounced with no previous discussion about what is likely to happen. Most families are able to produce a happy medium, with their child visiting the school during the previous term followed by occasional chats along the lines of 'When you start school . . .', backed up by library books which tell stories of children (or animals!) starting school and, of course, having a wonderful time when they get there. As the first day gets nearer, you can start to be more specific, mentioning the actual day (next Tuesday) and giving your child plenty of opportunities to ask questions and air any anxieties. If your preparation has gone well, your child should be looking forward to starting and should have a fairly good idea of what will happen there.

The night before

- Get everything ready the night before and encourage your child to help you put his clothes out and prepare his lunch box or snack. You will not want to rush your child in the morning as it can seem as if you cannot wait to get rid of him.
- Make sure he has already tried his uniform or any new clothes on and that everything is named, including his coat or anorak.
- Make sure your child goes to bed on time but do not give him an abnormally early night. If he is going to have to get up earlier than usual, start getting into the new routine at least a week before his first day.
- Make sure that your child is not exhausted by rushing around for the previous few days. At the same time, keep him occupied, so that he is not just sitting around waiting for school to start.
- Do not leave all the chats about anxieties and what is going to happen until the night before.

The first day

- Make sure your child has a good breakfast – at least a drink and a piece of toast if she is too excited for anything more.
- Leave plenty of time so that she does not feel rushed and so that she can dress herself as far as possible. If you do everything for her on the first morning, you will have set the pattern for doing it every time.
- If possible, team up with a friend and all walk or drive to school together. This will make the goodbyes easier.
- Make sure you already know which door you go in and where your child has to go.
- Make sure your child does not get there too early so that you

PREPARE YOUR CHILD FOR SCHOOL

have to hang around for ages outside the school or too late so that you both feel rushed and anxious.

- Do not be emotional or clingy yourself. It is a happy occasion and a positive step forward for your child.
- Give your child something new to take in on the first day such as crayons or a new school bag. You could give them to her on the first morning.

What to take

Uniform	Find out well in advance what the policy on uniform is. Many primary schools have an optional uniform so ask what percentage of first year pupils wear it. Your child will not want to feel different and you will not want to buy new clothes which do not get used.
Shoes	Ask if your child needs gym shoes to change into when he gets there.
Lunch box	Your child may have school dinners or come home at lunch time. Otherwise give him a sensible packed lunch including a piece of fruit and a high energy snack such as a muesli bar. Make sure that he can undo his flask and box easily for maximum independence.
Gym kit	Your child is unlikely to need this on the first day but find out well in advance what he will need for games and gym.
School bag	This may not be essential but is useful as your child will be bringing pictures, and later a reading book, home. Make sure that your child does not pack it full of his own toys to take to school. These tend to get lost

A photograph	or muddled up with another child's toys. Make sure you take a snap of your child on her first day. After all, it is a very special occasion.

Phased entry

Some schools operate a phased entry system so that new school entrants do not all start on the same day. This may involve your child starting a few days or weeks later than others in the same class. This will not put him at a disadvantage as the first few weeks are usually treated as a settling in period during which the teacher will informally assess your child, get to know him and help build up his confidence in the new situation.

A phased entry can involve a gradual build up of the time your child spends at school. So some children just go during the mornings to start with while others from the same class just attend the afternoon sessions. Again, this gives the teacher more time with individual children and gives your child a chance to settle in before being part of a larger group. You will be informed of the entry system when your child is offered a place at the school.

Busy doing 'nothing'

Ask your child what she did at school and you are very likely to get the answer – 'nothing'. But nothing could be further from the truth. One of the most important aims for the first term is for your child to settle in and feel positive about attending school. If she enjoys school then she will learn. The activities will be a continuation from nursery school or playgroup to start with. Your child will still mainly be learning through experience, experimentation and play so there is likely to be a sand tray, a water tray and a home corner in the classroom. Your child will continue with the creative activities she has been doing as a pre-schooler so expect paintings and the results of cutting and gluing activities to be brought home regularly. She will carry on with singing and music as well as physical activities which will now take the form of gym and organised games. Listening to stories will be an important part of the day and your child may watch educational television programmes or videos. Communication will be encouraged as children give their news and talk together in a structured way.

At the same time, some more formal activities will be started and you will recognise these as the first steps in reading, writing and maths. Many parents are in a rush to get their child started on reading, but do go along with the school on this. Do not be surprised if the first 'reading' book your child brings home has no words in it at all. Talking about the pictures and telling the story in her own words is an important first step for your child. However, by the end of the first term, most children will be attempting some form of formal reading which you can help with at home.

The National Curriculum

Before the introduction of the National Curriculum in 1988, it was left to schools and local authorities to decide what was taught. Now, children in state schools throughout England and Wales follow a similar curriculum and are assessed at specific ages. Private schools do not have to comply with the curriculum or carry out assessments, although many do. The first set assessment will take place when your child is seven but that does not mean that your teacher will not be assessing your child, albeit informally, as he progresses.

There are three core subjects to be studied – English, Maths and Science – and seven foundation subjects – Art, Technology, History, Geography, PE, a Foreign Language (from age 11) and Music. Your child will start work on the National Curriculum straight away but do not worry if it all sounds rather technical; experimenting with sand and water is Science and doing a project on your town or village is Geography. In the early stages, your child will not be taught in subjects but different topics will overlap during a variety of activities. If you look at the first set of attainment targets for reading, for example, you will see that your child will be working towards them straight away. They include recognising that print has meaning, developing an interest in books, talking about the content in stories and beginning to recognise individual words or letters in a familiar context. There are similar first attainments for writing, spelling, speaking and listening and for Maths and they are all within reach during the first year and sometimes during the first term.

Copies of the National Curriculum can be obtained at Her Majesty's Stationery Office (HMSO) book shops. The central address is at the back of the book. Scotland and Ireland have their own National Curricula.

Possible problems

Your child is bound to take time adjusting to her new routine. This adjustment should take place smoothly with few problems. However, many children will experience tiredness at the very least and others show signs of regressive or baby-like behaviour. These are quite normal although more serious problems in adjustment, resulting in reluctance to go to school, need careful handling and close liaison with the teachers.

Tiredness

This is very common, especially for children going straight into a full school day. Be very rigid about bed time during the first few weeks, with a long settling down period before your child goes to sleep. Your child may get over-excited about school and a warm bath and a quiet story should enable her to settle quickly. Your child may get grumpy as soon as she gets home so give her a high energy snack such as a muesli bar and let her do something undemanding like watching television. She may not be ready to talk about her school day straight away even though you are eager to hear all the details. Give her a chance to unwind first if she needs it.

Babyish behaviour

Some children show signs of regressive behaviour when they are confronted with anything new or demanding or when they have to get used to seeing less of you. Do not be surprised to see thumbs go back in and favourite soft toys reclaimed from the bottom of the toy basket. Your child may suddenly revert to a babyish voice or even start wetting the bed. Pay no attention to this as she is likely to get over it as she settles in at school. Never tell her off for regressive behaviour, just take it as a sign that your child needs a little extra attention and reassurance. If bed-wetting persists then check with her teacher to see if there are any problems at school and give your child plenty of opportunities to talk about any anxieties she may have.

Coughs and colds

It is not unusual for children to get more coughs and colds than ever before during their first winter at school. This is most common in children with little experience in a pre-school group. Always keep a close check on your child's ears and take her to your GP if she is in any pain or discomfort. Blocked or infected ears will affect your child's learning and concentration at school. If you are working, decide what arrangements you will make if your child is not well enough to attend school.

Aggression towards others

Your child may show aggression towards younger siblings at home, especially if you or your partner are staying at home to look after them. Make sure you give your child your full attention when she first comes home from school and if possible give her some time on her own at the end of the day. Do not make *your* day sound too interesting; instead put the focus on what your child has been doing at school. Remind her that the younger children will be going to school when they are older and emphasise how much they have missed her.

Aggression at school

It is very upsetting to hear that your child is being aggressive towards or picking on other children. Try not to get angry as it is as usually a sign that something is wrong. It could be that your child has low self-esteem and feels helpless and isolated. She then tries to cover up these feelings by making others feel the same. So try to find out if anything is worrying your child or if she has been having difficulty relating to the other children. While you try and boost her self-confidence discuss how the victim must be feeling. Encourage friendships by inviting one or two class mates home to play; this can include the children your child has been teasing or picking on. If the teasing is aggressive, make sure that you are not setting a bad example by being aggressive at home yourself.

Teasing

Most children will get teased by other children at some time but those who are not bothered by it and can brush it aside are unlikely to be picked on consistently. A likely victim is a child who is sensitive and emotional and who will react to teasing by crying. Teasing can become bullying if it is extreme either emotionally or physically. Bullying can happen even in the early primary years although it is more likely to be picked up quickly by parents and teachers than at secondary school.

If your child is withdrawn and upset or reluctant to go to school, talk to him and his teacher to see if he is getting teased or bullied. Discuss ways of dealing with teasing with your child. Point out that no one teases the furniture because it does not cry or react. Then discuss the benefits of ignoring the bully and walking away. If your child is being teased about something in particular such as wearing glasses, work out a reply for him to say; something like 'Four eyes are better than two' or 'You're just jealous'. Boost your child's confidence at home by praising his efforts and his appearance. Remind him how much you love and like him. If your child is used to gentle and humorous teasing at home, he is less likely to over-react to teasing at school. Also make sure that he hears you playfully teasing your partner who then laughs it off. However, if the teasing at school turns to bullying, you should go straight to the teacher to discuss it calmly.

Bad habits

You may feel that you have lost control of your child in some way as other people, both teachers and children, now have an influence on his behaviour. Hopefully these new influences will be mainly positive. However, he may pick up new words, expressions and behaviour which you know he has copied from other children and wish he had not. You are likely to hear his first swear words, rude songs and 'sloppy speech' during the first year at school. Your child will certainly try you out to see how you react so after pointing out calmly that certain words are not used in front of adults, try then to ignore them. Your child will gradually develop two codes of speech and will learn to keep the playground talk for when he is with his friends.

School refusal

If your child is reluctant to go to school or if she tries to avoid it with fake tummy aches, then there is certainly something wrong which needs sorting out. It may not be just a matter of waiting for her to settle in and grow out of it. Firstly, talk to your child's teacher to see if there is anything wrong at school. If the teacher has not noticed anything in particular, she will keep a close eye on your child as it may be something which occurs at a specific time of day. Perhaps, for example, she is frightened of the toilets or finds play time particularly difficult. What might seem like a small problem to us can be a very big one to a five-year-old. Never give in to your child's school refusal – make it absolutely clear that children have to attend school. However, talk to her about it and try to get to the root of the problem as soon as possible.

Changes for the better

Although your child may take time to settle down at school, after the first term you will already notice positive changes in her. She may suddenly seem to grow up and will certainly become more independent. Allow these changes to happen and ensure that you do not, quite unconsciously, try to keep your child as the young pre-schooler she once was, particularly if she is your youngest child.

Independence

Keep praising your child's efforts at independent skills. By the end of the term, she should be dressing and undressing herself quite efficiently. She should also be able to cope very well without you but will need your support and encouragement more than ever.

Eagerness to learn

One of the teacher's first aims, and yours, is to motivate your child. She should be eager to learn and be proud of her achievements.

New friends

Your child will be making friends who will last for years. There are bound to be arguments and one day she will say 'I'm never speaking to Fiona again' and the next day, they will be best friends. Your child is learning important social skills through building friendships. Never interfere with your child's choice of friends or criticise other children in front of her.

Maturity

Your child will suddenly seem to grow up. With her new friends, relationships with different adults and independent skills, you will begin to wonder if she needs you at all! Allow your child to mature, and enjoy the extra freedom which you too will have. At the same time, do not expect too much too soon – there will be a lot of things for a five-year-old to cope with and at times you will be reminded that she *is* only five.

Dealing with teachers and head teachers

- Do not try and have long conversations with your child's teacher as she is saying goodbye to all the children. If you have a problem which needs more than one or two minutes' chat, ask her when it would be convenient to speak to her.
- Try not to discuss your child in front of him.
- Start by asking for the teacher's advice. Try not to accuse her of anything (such as picking on your child) without knowing her opinion and the full facts first.
- Do tell the teacher when things are going right as well as when they are going wrong.
- Do attend parents' evenings and write down any questions you want to ask in advance.

- Go to the class teacher first if there is a problem. However, if you are not satisfied, consult the head teacher. If the problem is serious, it may be appropriate to see the class teacher and head teacher together.
- Do not criticise the teacher in front of your child.
- Do ask the teacher what you can do to help at home.

How to help at home

- Do go along with the work your child is being given. Do not try and push your child ahead with things she is not yet doing at school. If you feel the work is too easy or are eager for her to start specific tasks such as reading, discuss it with the teacher first. If you are still not satisfied, go to the head teacher. Do not be tempted to rush out and buy all the work books and reading books to get your child ahead.
- At first, school will be enough for your child without doing anything extra at home. However, do not forget that a walk in the forest, drawing pictures or even a trip to the shops is still educational.
- The first work that is likely to come home is a reading book, with or without words. Share your child's enthusiasm and praise all her efforts but never force her to do it. Give her enough help so that she always feels successful. If you are not sure what to do, always consult the teacher.
- Reinforce anything that your child is doing at school. So, for example, if she does a project on trees, go for a walk in the woods. Or if she is learning her numbers, point them out on doors or in books.
- If your child seems to have a particular difficulty with something, ask the teacher how you can help at home or if there is anything you could buy or borrow which would help.

Safety first

By the time your child starts school, he should already know how to cross the road, how to say no to strangers and about dangers in the home – so that he will not play with matches for example. However, you will probably still be using preventative measures such as child-proof lids and walking your child to and from school.

Road safety

If you live within easy walking distance of the school, you may want to start working towards your child walking to school without you. This would be better with other children rather than completely alone and can only be done when your child is ready. In the meantime, as you walk to school, talk about how and where to cross the road, gradually letting your child make the decisions about whether it is safe to cross, under your supervision. Encourage your child to listen as well as look both ways, and point out how dangerous it is crossing next to a parked car. If there is a pelican crossing or lollipop man, make it a rule to cross there even if cutting across elsewhere would be slightly quicker.

Stranger danger

Have very specific rules about this and a clear definition of what a stranger is.

Stranger danger guidelines

- Make it clear that a stranger is not just an odd-looking man in a mack. Strangers can be very friendly, pleasant-looking men and women who want to give sweets to children.
- Tell your child that a stranger who knows her name is still a stranger.

STARTING SCHOOL – THE FIRST TERM

- Tell your child:
  never to take sweets or presents from strangers;
  never to get into anyone's car without asking a parent
  first (even if it is someone she knows);
  never to go anywhere without asking a parent first.
- Always know where your child is and make sure she
  knows where you are.

Late-coming plan

Have a plan for if you are late arriving to collect your child
from school. Anyone can get stuck in a traffic jam so remind
your child what the plan is every now and then.

- Your child may have to stay with the teacher until you
  are there. If not, she should go back into the school,
  find a member of staff and tell her that you have not
  yet arrived.
- She should not hang around waiting outside the school.
- She should not get a lift home with anyone else unless
  it has been previously arranged by you. Always inform
  the school if anyone else is collecting your child and if
  you are held up, try to telephone.

Parents and teachers say . . .

❝ One new entrant came in to announce that Mummy
had had a baby girl. This news came every morning
for ten days. Each time the older sister denied it.
Two weeks later a baby boy was born and the child
came in and said nothing! ❞

    Mandy Catto, early stages class teacher, Westhill

❝ One child had not had any experience in a nursery
or playgroup. She had never seen or handled some

PREPARE YOUR CHILD FOR SCHOOL

of the materials before and became quite obsessed with the novelty of Plasticine. On frequent occasions, a long trail of Plasticine led to her chair! She found it very difficult to share with others and was very demanding of my attention.

Sheila Reidford, infant teacher, Monymusk

When I asked my five-year-old what the best thing about his first day had been, he thought very carefully and said "Going home". Happily, his teacher informed me that he had been happy and settled all day.

Carol White, Aberdeen

Remember that not all children in a class are ready to start formal learning at the same time. Because of this, children will be taught in groups. Once all the children have been admitted to a class, the class teacher will draw up the initial groups, based on her assessment carried out during the phased entry.

Induction booklet for Mile End School, Aberdeen

On the first day, Christopher happily informed me that he had done "nothing". On the second day, I asked him again, what he had been doing to which he replied "The same as yesterday".

Lindsay Kennedy, Stonehaven

Useful addresses

British Association for Early Childhood Education, Studio 32, 140 Tabernacle Street, London EC2A 4SD (Tel 071 7397594).

Campaign for the Advancement of State Education (CASE), The Grove, 110 High Street, Sawston, Cambs, CB2 4HJ (Tel 0223 833179).

Education Otherwise, PO Box 120, Leamington Spa, Warwickshire, CV32 7ER (Tel 0926 886828).

Fit Kids Ltd, The Lodge, Bakery Place, Altenburg Gardens, Clapham, London SW11 1JQ (Tel 071 9244435).

Her Majesty's Stationery Office (HMSO), PO Box 276, London SW8 5DT (Tel 071 8739090).

Hyperactive Children's Support Group, 71 Whyke Lane, Chichester, Sussex (Tel 0903 725182).

Independent Schools Information Service (ISIS), 56 Buckingham Gate, London SW1 6AG (Tel 071 6308793).

Montessori Centre, 18 Balderton Street, London W1Y 1TG (Tel 071 4930165).

National Association For Gifted Children, 1 South Audley Street, London W1Y 5DQ (Tel 071 4991188).

National Confederation of Parent–teacher Associations, 2 Ebsfleet Industrial Estate, Stonebridge Road, Gravesend, Kent DA11 9DZ (Tel 0474 560618).

National Curriculum Council, 15–17 New Street, York, YO1 2RA (Tel 0904 622533).

Pre-School Playgroups Association, 61–63 Kings Cross Road, London WC1X 9LL (Tel 071 833 0991).

Pre-School Playgroups Association (Scotland), 14 Elliot Place, Glasgow G3 8EP (Tel 041 2214148).

Toy Libraries Association (Playmatters), Seabrooks House, Wyllotts Manor, Darkes Lane, Potters Bar, Herts EN6 2HL.

Tumble Tots Bluebird Park, Bromsgrove Road, Hunnington, Halesowen, West Midlands B62 0JW (Tel 021 585 7003).

Index

A

After-school clubs 134
Age of school entry 139
Aggression 89, 105, 159
Anxieties 158
Appeals for school entry 136
Applications for school places 135
Assessment 5
Attention span 70
Auditory memory 43

B

Bad habits 104, 160
Bed-wetting 147
Behaviour 92, 98, 99
Books 85, 88, 118
British Association for Early
    Childhood Education 112,
    167
Bullying 105

C

Catchment areas 131
Child minders 111
Church schools 140
Class sizes 133
Clinical medical officer 145
Clumsy children 28
Colour 26
Comforters 53
Computers 90
Concentration 10
Confidence 57
Conversation 19
Copying 124
Counting 126

D

Deafness 79
Decision making 64
Delayed school entry 147

Development assessment 5
Discipline 134
Drawing 124
Dressing 60
Dyslexia 128

E

Education Act 1981 146
Education authorities 111
Education Otherwise 138, 167
Educational psychologist 145
Equipment 81, 113, 133
Emotional difficulties 147
Eye–hand co-ordination 123

F

Families 4
Family therapy 147
Fire safety 11
First day 153
First term 152
Four- to five-year-olds 30
Friends 4, 92, 162

G

Glasses 65
Goodbyes 46
Grammar 19, 21, 35
Gym 154

H

Hand control 123
Head teachers 133, 162
Hearing loss 5
Health visitors 5, 144
Her Majesty's Stationery Office 167
Home teaching 138
Hyperactive Children's Support
    Group 80, 167
Hyperactivity 76

I

Imaginary friends 105
Imagination 42
Independence 9, 59, 65, 161
Independent schools 137
Independent Schools Information
    Service (ISIS) 137, 167
Independent Schools Year Book
    137
Induction booklet 150
Infant schools 139
Infections 158
Instructions 72

J

Junior schools 139

L

Late coming plan 165
Laterality 129
Learning difficulties 146

Learning support 134
Left-handedness 129
Letters 121
Libraries 88
Listening 10, 69
Lying 103

M

Manipulation 16, 33
Matching 120, 125
Manners 104
Maths 125
Maturity 162
Memory 43, 121
Middle school 139
Mirrors 39
Montessori Centre 112, 167
Montessori Nurseries 109
Mother and toddler groups 115
Motivation 162
Movement 8, 14, 31
Moving house 140

N

National Association for Gifted
    Children 168
National Confederation of Parent–
    teacher Associations 168
National Curriculum 137, 156
National Curriculum Council 168
Nose-blowing 63
Numbers 127

Nursery classes 108
Nursery nurses 110
Nursery rhymes 19, 35
Nursery schools 108
Nursery teachers 5

O

Open-plan schools 141
Opportunity groups 117

P

Paediatricians 28, 145
Parent–teacher associations 134
Parental involvement 134
Pencil control 123
Pencil grips 130
Phased entry 155
Physical development 8, 14, 31
Physical difficulties 146
Play 8, 9, 24, 40
Play matters 168
Playgroup leaders 5
Playgroups 110, 116
Pre-prep school 140
Pre-maths 125
Pre-reading 10
Pre-school assessment 142
Pre-School Playgroups Association
    111, 116, 168
Pre-writing 10
Preparatory school 137, 140
Preparatory School Year Book 137

Prepositions 19, 21
Pretend play 25, 41, 42
Primary school 132
Private nurseries 109
Private schools 137
Progress 135
Pronouns 19
Prospectus 132
Psychological service 147
Puzzles 40

Q

Qualifications 114
Questions 19

R

Reading 118, 163
Reading schemes 91
Reception classes 139
Regressive behaviour 68, 158
Religion 136
Remedial teaching 145
Reports 135
Rising five groups 117
Road safety 164
Routine 153
Rules 81

S

Safety 11, 85, 164
School refusal 161
Scissors 33, 34

Self-help skills 59
Sentences 35
Separation 46
Shapes 126
Sharing 96
Shyness 55
Siblings 159
Sight 5
Singing 19, 41
Size 21, 126
Slow learners 134
Social services 111
Social skills 9, 92
Sorting 125
Special needs 145
Speech and language 5
Speech and language therapy 28, 29
Stammering 28
Star charts 52
Statements of special needs 145
Stories 71, 119
Stranger danger 164
Swearing 160
Swimming 15

T

Talking 7, 19, 35
Teachers 133, 162
Teasing 159
Telephone 35
Television 90
Tenses 19

INDEX

Three- to four-year-olds 13
Time 37
Tiredness 157
Toilet 62
Toy libraries 91
Toy Library Association 91, 168
Toys 41, 81
Tracing 129, 124
Turn taking 95

U

Understanding 8, 21, 37
Uniform 135, 154

V

Visiting nurseries 114
Visiting schools 132
Visual skills 9, 23, 39
Vocabulary 19, 35
Voluntary-aided schools 140

W

Working parents 49, 112
Writing 123, 125